ABOUT THE AUTHOR

Tammy Garner began her artistic journey in early childhood and has worked with a variety of mediums over the years. She started working in polymer clay in 1994 and metal clay in 2004, with her main focus on jewelry.

She received her certification in Precious Metal Clay in 2007. Her work has been featured in *Polymer Clay Creative Traditions* by Judy Belcher, private and public art showings and has won several awards. She is a member of the PMC Guild, National Polymer Clay Guild, the West Virginia Art and Craft Guild and is currently the president of the Kanawha Valley Polymer Clay Guild.

Tammy is a metal clay and polymer clay instructor who also dabbles in sterling silver, copper, enamel, fused glass, fibers and paint. She proudly retails her works of art under the name a Peace of Art. She resides in St. Albans, West Virginia, with her husband, Jerry, daughter, Scarlet, and her two feline companions.

ACKNOWLEDGMENTS

I would like to thank North Light Books for giving me this fabulous, and unexpected, opportunity to write this book. Thanks to some of my wonderful mentors—Olivia, Kim, Judy and Marcia—for so graciously believing in my work and always trying to push me, sometimes kicking and screaming, down that professional artist's path. Without them and my other artsy pals (you know who you are) I definitely would not be where I am today.

I want to give a big thanks to Jennifer Claydon, Christine Polomsky and Amanda Dalton for being so kind, generous and a laugh-a-minute while listening to all my corny jokes and "Tammyisms." They are my forever and only "Tree Stick Pals."

I definitely want to thank all the companies that kindly donated materials for this book, and they are PMC Supply; Art Clay World USA; Polyform Products; Ranger Industries; Rupert, Gibbon & Spider, Inc., manufacturer of Jacquard Products; Artistic Wire Ltd.; and Henkel Corporation, manufacturer of Loctite Products. I appreciate their generosity, and I will continue to work with and promote their products.

DEDICATION

I would like to dedicate this book to a few. To God, for granting me peace in my heart and blessing me with this wonderful gift that I can share with others. To my late father, who kept me supplied with all the markers, crayons, paper and love a child could ever want, and who instilled in me the desire to always strive for perfection. To my mother, who raised me to be a strong, independent and unselfish individual, and who taught me to never hide in the shadows but to always jump out in front and "shine." To my husband, who, ever so quietly, allows me to remain on that road of "artistic ambition" by continuing my art education instead of refining my domestic skills. To my baby girl, a teenager and "closet artist," who agrees to help burnish, sand or string beads if she can talk on the phone while doing so. To my brother, an exceptional musician, who always supports me and thinks all my work is "really cool" even when, sometimes, it's not. I love you all!

contents

EARRINGS
FOR EVERYONE

38

NOTABLE
NECKWEAR

66

BRACELETS, RINGS
& OTHER THINGS

96

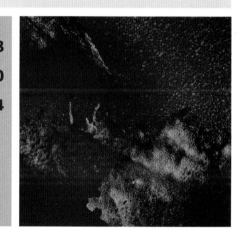

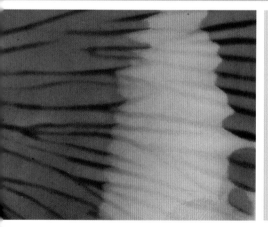

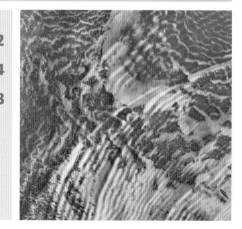

INTRODUCTION

Metal clay. Maybe you have heard about it. Maybe you have worked with it. Maybe you have a package of it stored away in a dark corner of your craft room and you're too intimidated to open it. Or, maybe you have no idea what I am talking about. And maybe, just maybe … well, I've run out of maybes. But, if you fall into any of those categories, you will find information and projects within this book that are sure to pique your interest.

You see, metal clay is not just for those artsy-fartsy people that have already mastered the art of making jewelry. Instead, it can be used and appreciated by everyone, from beginning crafters to skilled jewelers. I should know, because I fall somewhere in the middle of that spectrum. If you peruse magazines about making your own jewelry, you will notice evidence of the increasing popularity of this medium, as more and more pieces of featured jewelry include metal clay components. But the accompanying statements about "this remarkable and unconventional new way to work with metal" can be a bit intimidating. This book is designed to make working with metal clay approachable, affordable and fun.

Working with this fascinating material is simpler than you might imagine. Metal clay consists of only three elements: metal particles, binder and water. Are you wondering how it ends up as a solid piece of metal if it starts out as a pliable clay? It has to do with the firing process. When metal clay is heated to a specific temperature the organic binder burns off and the metal particles sinter, or fuse, to one another, making a solid piece of metal. At that point, the piece is 99.9 percent fine silver that can be treated like any other piece of fine silver. Contrary to popular belief, though, you don't need a kiln to perform this magic. Every project in this book can be hand-fired with a simple butane torch.

Making beautiful metal clay jewelry is really just a matter of opening the package of clay, texturing it, then cutting and firing it. A few more steps can be added for fancier results, but the whole process is very easy to learn and doesn't have to be time intensive. Of course, it goes without saying that some techniques take a bit of practice. Once you've mastered them, you can move on to more complicated projects beyond those featured in this book. *Metal Clay in a Day* will introduce you to this medium with stylish projects that are fun and easy—and I've included a big dose of humor to go along with them.

See, not so intimidating now, is it?

Working with Metal Clay

MATERIALS

Let's begin by talking about the basic materials you will need (and a few other things you may want) to make metal clay jewelry. Any tools you don't have on hand will usually be affordable and easy to find, but you probably already have the basic necessities right in your own home.

ABOUT METAL CLAY

Metal clay: What exactly is it? Well, I had an instructor tell me, "It's really not a clay at all; it's fine silver!" This sounded better to me at the time, and people seem to understand that better when I describe my work to them.

Not to get too scientific, but metal clay is … drum roll please … precious metal particles (either silver or gold) suspended in a nontoxic organic binder with water. The metal particles in metal clay are so small that it would take as many as twenty-five particles fused together to equal the size of a grain of salt. The resulting mixture is very pliable and can be manipulated like clay by rolling, stamping, cutting, texturing, sculpting and molding. When the clay is dried and fired at a high temperature, the binder burns off and the metal particles sinter (or fuse together), creating a solid piece of metal that can be manipulated like other fine metals. Voila! a beautiful piece of fine silver jewelry right there in your hands (after it cools, of course).

There are two brands of metal clay on the market today. The two are very similar in both their working properties and finished result. Both brands offer several forms and varieties of clay to choose from. The projects in this book are all made from low-fire clay that can be fired with a handheld butane torch.

Precious Metal Clay

Precious Metal Clay, also known as PMC, is manufactured by Mitsubishi Materials Corporation in Japan. It was developed in the early 1990s and introduced to the United States in 1996. Mitsubishi manufactures gold metal clay (22K) and silver metal clay (.999FS). PMC is available in four varieties.

PMC Standard is the original type of fine silver metal clay made by Mitsubishi. Compared to newer varieties of metal clay, it contains a high percentage of water and binder, making it more pliable with a longer working time than other metal clays. It is a good clay to use for small items, carved items and items with great detail. It is not a good choice for larger items or pieces that will get a lot of wear because it is the least dense metal clay available. PMC Standard has a shrinkage rate of 25 to 30 percent.

PMC+ is a good all-purpose fine silver metal clay for earrings, brooches, pendants, beads and charms. It contains less water and binder than PMC Standard. Denser and stronger than PMC Standard, it has a shrinkage rate of 10 to 15 percent.

PMC3 is a strong fine silver metal clay with a low firing point. It is great for earrings, brooches, pendants, beads and charms, as well as rings and pieces that will get a lot of wear and need strength. It is also the ideal clay for adding stones or glass, and it does well with torch firing. Of the metal clays, it contains the smallest amount of water and binder. It is also the densest metal clay, with a shrinkage rate of 10 to 12 percent. I used this clay to create all of the projects in this book.

PMC Gold is a good clay for earrings, brooches, pendants and beads. It can be fired together with fine silver metal clay. After firing, the metal that remains is 22K gold with a similar density to PMC3. It has a shrinkage rate of 14 to 19 percent.

Art Clay

Art Clay is manufactured by Aida Chemical Industries in Japan. They began manufacturing metal clay in 1991. They manufacture gold metal clay (22K) and silver metal clay (.999FS). Art Clay is available in four varieties.

Standard Art Clay Silver is a good all-purpose clay for earrings, brooches, pendants, beads and charms. It can be fired with glass and some stones. The shrinkage rate is 8 to 12 percent.

Standard Art Clay Silver Slow Dry contains a special binder that keeps it moist for a longer working time. It is good for rings and items with fine details. This variety of clay should not be mixed with other types of clay due to the difference in the binder. The shrinkage rate is 8 to 12 percent.

Art Clay Silver 650/1200 has the lowest firing point of any Art Clay. It works well when you want to include sterling silver findings when firing. It can be fired with glass, some stones and ceramics. This clay shrinks a bit less than the other types, at a rate of 8 to 9 percent.

Art Clay Gold is a good clay for earrings, brooches, pendants and beads. After firing, the metal is 22K gold.

Forms

Metal clay is available in several different forms. Each form has its own important place in metal clay work. Make sure to use the different forms properly, and you will have beautiful, long-lasting projects.

Lump clay is the moldable, pliable form used for most projects. It is available in assorted gram-weight packages and needs no prior conditioning.

Syringe clay is a soft version of lump clay in a ready-to-use extruder. Use it to fill cracks, join pieces of metal clay together and make decorative elements and surface designs.

Paste is metal clay that has been thinned with water to the consistency of toothpaste that can be applied with a small paintbrush or palette knife. It can be used to fill cracks, create surface designs and join metal clay parts together. Paste can be thinned with water to form slip, a liquid metal clay that forms weaker connections than paste.

Oil paste is metal clay that has been thinned with oil to a toothpaste consistency that can be applied with a small paintbrush or palette knife. It is great for joining broken items fired or unfired—and filling unwanted cracks. Oil paste is currently available only in Art Clay Silver.

Sheet (or paper) clay is a thin, flexible, almost rubbery type of metal clay that will not dry out. It can be folded (to create origami) or cut with scissors or paper punches. Sheets can be sealed together with a bit of water to make thicker sheets. This form of clay is great for decorative elements.

tip

A good way to store metal clay and paste for later use is to keep it in an airtight plastic container. Place a small damp sponge with a bit of vinegar on it inside the container. The sponge holds moisture in the container and the vinegar helps discourage mold. Keep the container in a cool area away from heat. Check on the clay periodically if you are not using it, and add water as needed if the clay begins to dry out.

SETTING UP A WORK SPACE

So, you are eager to get started—but where should you work? You can actually set up a nice little work space right at your kitchen table without forcing your family to eat on the porch. You may find you already have some of the following items on hand. If not, don't worry; they're easy to find.

A hard surface is preferred for rolling out level sheets of clay. Any flat, smooth tabletop or countertop will do. A sheet of glass or Plexiglas also works wonderfully. If you find yourself in a pinch, you can use the bottom of a glass baking dish, a flat ceramic platter or a piece of glass out of a picture frame. When working with metal clay, avoid aluminum pans and foil, as aluminum can have a negative reaction and cause the metal in the clay to discolor. If you aren't working directly on a tabletop or countertop, I recommend a few pieces of tape to keep your work surface from slipping while you work.

A flexible surface placed on top of the hard surface is necessary when working with wet clay. By sliding the flexible surface to the edge of your hard surface and bending it, you can lift your wet clay piece off the flexible surface without distorting its form. I suggest using a plastic sheet protector on top of the hard surface in your work space. You can find them at any store that carries school or office supplies. I also like to insert graph paper marked with 8 × 8 squares per inch (3 × 3 squares per centimeter) into the sheet protector to help with measuring.

A plastic cup is very useful to serve as a humidifier cup for your stored clay scraps. Metal clay contains water, and in order to handle the clay easily, you must keep it moist at all times. When you are working on a project you will accumulate scrap pieces of clay along the way. You can put those pieces back into the original clay package or use a small plastic condiment cup, spritzed with water, as a humidifier to place over the scraps until you are through with your project. (You can find plastic condiment cups at most any restaurant, usually with salad dressing or other sauces in them.) A single-serving applesauce cup works nicely as well. This is a great way to recycle!

Plastic wrap is an item I cannot do without. I keep a 6" × 6" (15cm × 15cm) piece of plastic wrap (any brand will do) on top of my flexible surface for covering my clay while working. Covering the clay while you are not working on it will help keep it moist, especially if you roll a sheet but have to stop for a moment to find a tool. Always remember to keep the clay covered.

WORKING WITH WET CLAY

The most important thing I have to say about working with fresh metal clay: hydration, hydration, hydration! One thing that seems to discourage potential metal clay addicts is the clay losing too much moisture too soon, making the clay difficult to work with. By just following a few easy guidelines, you should have no problem with premature … uh … evaporation! Here are some basic items needed for properly manipulating fresh clay. These items are fairly common, and a quick trip to your local grocery or craft store should help you obtain anything you don't already have.

Olive oil or balm should be used to keep metal clay from sticking to your hands and tools while you are working. It is a good idea to lightly coat just about anything that will be touching the metal clay, including your hands, with an oil or balm. Badger Balm is used by many metal clay artists and is widely available. I prefer to make my own hand balm (see recipe on page 125) because I can customize it by adding whatever scent I desire.

Water is vital to successfully working with metal clay. I like to keep a small spray bottle of water on hand to lightly spritz the clay, humidifier cup or paste as needed. I also keep a small plastic jar of water for washing my paintbrushes. I prefer distilled water as it is free of contaminants.

A roller is used to form the metal clay into thin sheets. I recommend using a piece of PVC pipe in a small diameter, cut to approximately 6" (15cm) long. PVC pipe is easy to find at any hardware store. In a pinch, a straight-sided drinking glass, a smooth round pen, or a Plexiglas roller for polymer clay can also be used.

Playing cards can be used to measure the thickness of a metal clay sheet (a method developed by Tim McCreight). When you roll out a sheet of clay, lay an equal number of playing cards in a stack on each side of the clay for the roller to rest on to give you a smooth, even sheet of clay. You can also cut and stack a few strips from a cereal box or any other thin cardboard if you don't have cards on hand.

A tissue blade or a craft knife is a handy tool for cutting through metal clay. To get a perfectly straight cut, the best tool for the job is a tissue blade, which resembles an oversized razor blade. A craft knife works well for cutting shapes freehand. Both tools can be found at a local craft or hardware store. If they are not readily available, try using a paring knife. Always use extreme caution when working with any knife or blade.

A needle tool or toothpick can be used in many ways when working with metal clay. A needle tool can be used instead of a craft knife to cut metal clay as it has no blade edge and can therefore cut in any direction. It can also be used to make holes and draw designs into wet clay or scratch marks onto dry clay. Needle tools are available at craft stores and at shops where ceramic and pottery supplies are sold. Although a toothpick is not as sharp as a needle tool, it is great for making holes in wet clay, as well as for making impressions or supporting small tubes of clay.

Paintbrushes are used to brush water, slip and paste onto metal clay. If any metal clay dries on your brush, simply clean it with water.

A ruler is handy for measuring the clay as you work. Having a marked grid on your flexible work surface can be helpful for measurements, as well.

ADDING TEXTURES AND PATTERNS

One of the great things about metal clay is how well it will accept texture and form. There are many ways you can give your jewelry a unique design; once you start looking for textures you will be amazed at how many are all around you. To texture metal clay you can use many commercial products, such as rubber stamps, texture sheets or metal stamping tools. But if you are itching for a one-of-a-kind pattern for your piece, I recommend making your own texturing tools out of simple materials such as polymer clay, wire or household items. It is easier than you may think, and most of the time it is much more economical than using commercial tools.

Rubber stamps can be pressed into metal clay to create a variety of textures and images. I prefer unmounted stamps when working with metal clay, as they are flexible and can be pressed into the clay with a roller. Rubber stamps can be found at numerous places, including craft and office supply stores.

Household items are a great resource for unique and inventive textures. Flatware, glassware, bottle and toothpaste caps, scrub pads, fabric, lace, buttons, old jewelry and much more can all be used to make impressions in metal clay. Nature also gives us an abundant array of textures and patterns, including leaves, tree bark, grass and other beautiful organic items. Keep your eyes peeled, and you'll find new textures for your projects everywhere.

Making your own texture items is also a great way to expand your horizons past commercial products. You can make textures and patterns by using simple tools you may already have on hand. Some of my favorites include carving a design into an eraser or polymer clay, carving a design into PVC pipe, or using glue or dimensional paint to create a design on a wood block or cardboard. I also enjoy making designs with 16- or 18-gauge wire that can be pressed into metal clay. The possibilities are as varied as your imagination allows.

Layering clay elements also creates new textures and patterns that you can't acheive with a single layer of clay. Metal clay paste can make an interesting texture when a palette knife is used to spread or glob it onto a piece. The metal clay in syringes can be used to create ropes of metal clay. Metal clay sheet or paper can be cut with regular or decorative scissors. Simply use metal clay paste or slip to join pieces of metal clay together.

Molds are widely used to duplicate shapes with metal clay. There are several types of mold-making materials on the market. Occasionally, I use a two-part molding compound; this is especially handy if you are traveling and you see an object or texture that you would love to duplicate. More often I use polymer clay to make molds because it is inexpensive and has a longer working time. The only downside to polymer clay molds is that they have to be baked (or cured) in an oven to harden.

WORKING WITH DRY CLAY

Once you have manipulated the wet metal clay into your chosen design, you must dry and refine the piece before it is ready for firing. As metal clay dries, it loses moisture and becomes lighter in color. There are two main drying stages of metal clay: leather hard and bone dry. The leather hard stage is when the clay is dry to the touch but still contains a bit of moisture. It can be decoratively carved or scratched, and it can easily be joined to other pieces of clay by using a bit of water. Before it is fired, the metal clay will need to continue drying until it reaches the bone dry (or completely dry) stage. At this stage, the metal clay will be free of moisture. Bone-dry clay is fairly fragile, but you can still drill it, scratch it and construct with it, in addition to sanding and filing it. Below are a few ways to dry a piece and some items for refining metal clay for a beautiful finish.

Drying

Time will end up drying clay all by itself. You can leave your piece to dry on your work space or on some other flat surface overnight. To help air circulate under your piece and to speed drying time, elevate the metal clay by placing it on a dry sponge or a drying rack made of mesh.

A drying box made from a cardboard box and a hair dryer can be used to dry metal clay quickly. Start by cutting a hole—slightly larger than the barrel of the hair dryer—in the center of one side of a cardboard box. Turn the box on its side so the hole is on top and the box opening is to the side. Insert the barrel of the hair dryer into the hole; tape it to the box if needed to hold it in place. Place a drying rack or dry sponge on the bottom of the box to hold the metal clay as it dries. Never leave an active drying box unattended.

A mug warmer is like a miniature hot plate and can very quickly dry metal clay. Inexpensive mug warmers or candle warmers can be purchased at many craft and retail stores. I suggest using a pair of tweezers to lift a dried piece of clay off the warmer as the clay will get very hot. Do not leave an operating mug warmer unattended.

Refining

Nail files and emery boards are handy for refining dried metal clay. Once the metal clay dries, all rough edges and corners need to be smoothed out before the piece is fired. Starting out, I recommend a four-in-one file that includes four different grits all in one handy file. This can be purchased at any large retail store or salon supply store.

Sandpaper can also be used to smooth dried clay and can be quite useful for reaching places where files don't fit. I recommend wet/dry sandpaper because it is a little more flexible than other types of sandpaper and it comes in a variety of grits. Start with a 400–500 grit for removing large amounts of clay and move up to a 1,000-grit sandpaper for fine smoothing.

A craft knife can be used for drilling and cleaning up holes in dried clay and also for light carving. Craft knives are easy to find in hardware or craft stores. They are inexpensive and usually come with extra blades.

FIRING

Now it is time to magically turn your interesting lump of clay into a beautiful piece of silver. For the silver to sinter together, metal clay needs to reach a certain temperature and then stay at that temperature for a specific time. The firing chart below will help you determine how long your project will need to be fired. There are several ways to fire your piece and several products on the market you can use.

A firing surface is a fireproof object to place your clay piece on for firing. I recommend using a soldering board; however a simple firebrick is easier to obtain and will do just as well. Firebricks are fairly cheap and designed to withstand high temperatures. They can be purchased at a brick and block or masonry store. While firing, set your firing surface on top of a heatproof surface, such as a stove top so your clay piece does not cause damage if if happens to roll off the brick while still hot.

A butane torch can be used to fire all of the projects in this book. Torch firing works best on pieces that weigh 25 grams or less. A butane torch puts the power right into your hands. Also called kitchen or crème brûlée torches, these are available starting at $20 at kitchen supply stores, home improvement stores and some craft or retail stores. Butane refills can be purchased at a grocery or retail store.

A gas stove can also be used to fire metal clay. Place the metal clay on a piece of stainless steel mesh on top of the burner. The flame from the gas stove works similar to the torch flame: You'll need to adjust it to control the heat.

A timer is handy to have on hand to track your firing time. Once the metal clay has reached sintering temperature, start your timer and hold the metal clay at the sintering temperature for the length of time indicated in the firing chart below.

Safety is a very important consideration whenever you work with fire. With any firing device, read the manufacturer's instructions before attempting to use the item. I recommend having a fire extinguisher and a pair of leather safety gloves on hand, just in case. Remember, this is metal and it gets very hot when fired. Accidents can happen and I have the holes in my studio floor to prove it! As they say, "It's all fun and games until…" well, you know the rest.

metal clay torch firing chart

CLAY TYPE	CLAY WEIGHT 1-5 GRAMS	CLAY WEIGHT 6-15 GRAMS	CLAY WEIGHT 16-25 GRAMS	SHRINKAGE
Art Clay Silver Standard	1-1.5 minutes	1-1.5 minutes	2-4 minutes	8-12%
Art Clay Slow Dry	1.5 – 2 minutes	1.5 – 2 minutes	2-4 minutes	8-12%
Art Clay Silver 650/1200	1.5 – 2 minutes	1.5 – 2 minutes	2-4 minutes	8-9%
PMC+	5 minutes	5 minutes	5 minutes	10-15%
PMC3	2 minutes	2 minutes	3-5 minutes	10-12%

The times listed in this chart are minimums. It does not hurt the metal clay to be fired longer than the time shown.

BURNISHING

After firing, although the piece is 99.9 percent fine silver, it will have a white, matte appearance and won't look like silver at all. By burnishing the piece, you will truly see the transformation from clay to metal. Burnishing compresses the metal surface, pressing down all the unevenness in the metal, which allows it to reflect light and to shine. The more the silver is compressed, the shinier it looks. A couple of different tools can be used for this process.

A brass or stainless steel brush is the first item used in the burnishing process. Although I have had success with dry-brushing, I prefer to brush using water and a bit of liquid soap. This gives a piece a brushed satin finish. I recommend having a large brush to use on all of your pieces as well as a small brush for doing detail work. These brushes can be purchased at home improvement, automotive, variety and craft stores.

A nylon scrub pad can also be used to burnish a fired piece. Try using one after brush burnishing for a matte finish with fewer scratches than from brush burnishing alone.

A metal spoon is a great tool for further compressing the silver for a shinier finish. Using a spoon will especially highlight any raised portions of your design.

A silver-polishing cloth will further buff and polish your fired jewelry to a high shine. A chemical in most polishing cloths removes tarnish and shines the metal.

AFTER–FIRING TREATMENTS

After you have fired and burnished your silver piece, you can choose from several options for further beautification. There are many treatments you can apply to give it depth or add some color. These are just a few ideas on how you can jazz up or tone down your creation.

Liver of sulfur is my preferred method of patinating. The compound has a nasty odor, but it yields a beautiful range of colors. Follow the manufacturer's directions on the use and disposal of this product.

Oil paint can be used to create "patina in a pinch." Rub black oil paint firmly on the area you would like darkened and wipe the paint away from the raised areas.

Two-part epoxy can be mixed with paints, mica powders or inks and then be added to metal clay for a faux-enamel look. Epoxy is a two-part formula and is available in syringe or bottle form. Read the manufacturer's directions on mixing, and be sure to work in a well-ventilated area.

ADDITIONAL TOOLS AND MATERIALS YOU MAY WANT

Okay, you have made a few pieces out of metal clay and your jewelry looks stunning—but you feel an itching in your fingers. You have developed "MCS" (Metal Clay Syndrome). The only cure is to make more metal clay objects, which means you will probably want to add more tools and supplies to your tool kit. Most of these items will make your work with metal clay a bit easier and less time consuming and your projects more beautiful. Of course, because there is a plethora of items on the market, I cannot list them all, but here are some favorites.

Burnishers are handy little tools that are used to burnish the metal for a shiny finish. They come in different sizes in stainless steel and agate. Burnishers can be found at metal clay and jewelry suppliers.

Carving tools can be used for carving leather-hard clay. These are usually available at craft stores. Some dental tools are also nice for carving and scratching patterns into clay. I usually find these at my local flea market.

Cardstock is good for making templates. It is thick enough to reuse, and it is sturdier than text-weight paper.

Clay keepers are great for holding clay while you are working, or for long-term storage. They keep your clay moist; no rewrapping required. If you use different types of clay, I recommend using one labeled container for each type.

Clay shapers are rubber-tipped tools that are good for shaping and moving clay. These are also great for blending clay for invisible seams. Clay shapers come in a variety of sizes and shapes and can be purchased at art and craft stores and from metal clay and polymer clay suppliers.

Cork clay is a workable medium made of cork. Shape the cork clay as desired, let it dry thoroughly, then form the metal clay right around the cork form. When fired, the cork burns out, leaving a hollow form. I suggest using this for beads to conserve clay and to keep the weight of the beads to a minimum. Cork clay should only be fired in a kiln due to the fumes it emits. You can find cork clay at most metal clay supply stores.

Chlorine bleach is an inexpensive product that is easy to use to create a medium to dark gray patina on fine silver.

Drill bits are great for making holes in dried clay. A pin vise will hold different bit sizes and will provide a handle to hold while drilling.

A kiln is an oven specifically designed to reach and hold a high temperature for firing metal clay.

Magnifiers, or jeweler's loupes, are must-haves if you do a lot of small, fine work. You can find these at some art and craft stores or at jewelry supply stores.

Needle files are little files for use in small areas, and they can also be used for filing fired clay. Their prices vary depending on quality. I use the cheaper ones for filing and fine-tuning dry clay before I fire it. I use a better-quality set for filing rough edges or enlarging holes after firing. You'll find these at local tool stores as well as jewelry and metal clay suppliers.

Nonstick baking liners are reusable baking sheet and pan liners made of fiberglass coated with Teflon. These are great items to use as your flexible work surface.

Polishing papers come in different grits for use on dry or fired clay. I like to use these papers for a nice mirror finish on a metal clay piece. I buy a package that contains assorted grits from 400 to 4,000. I recommend trying several to see which ones work best for you. You can find these at jewelry and metal clay supply stores.

A shrinkage ruler has two sets of measurements. One side is a standard ruler, and the other side shows the measurement a piece will have after firing. This is great for getting the finished piece to the desired size. Shrinkage rulers can be found at some jewelry supply and metal clay supply stores.

A tumbler is a small machine that uses stainless steel shot to polish items. Using a tumbler takes the labor out of hand polishing and buffing your metal clay creations.

THE BASIC METAL CLAY TOOL KIT

Let's review the items needed for a basic metal clay tool kit. For every type of art or craft you should have a basic tool kit on hand for use with each project, and metal clay is no exception. You will only need a few items for your kit, and most of those can be kept nicely in a "ready for action" container. Your basic kit will include some items for your work space, some clay working tools and some refining and firing tools.

MATERIALS

WORK SPACE

hard surface

flexible surface

plastic wrap

humidifier cup

fire extinguisher

CLAY WORKING TOOLS

olive oil or beeswax balm

water

roller

tissue blade or craft knife

ruler

paintbrush

needle tool

toothpick

playing cards

REFINING & FIRING TOOLS

mug warmer

nail files

sandpaper

tweezers

butane torch

firing brick

brass brush

TECHNIQUES

Any art form has starting points, basic techniques you need to know for each creative journey. One of the interesting aspects of metal clay is that so many different techniques can be used to shape it. These basic how-to's will be the foundation of every metal clay project. I recommend reading through all of the techniques before beginning a project, so you will feel a bit surer of yourself when starting. Once you have practiced these techniques, you will probably feel comfortable enough to expand on them, letting your imagination run wild with ideas for other pieces.

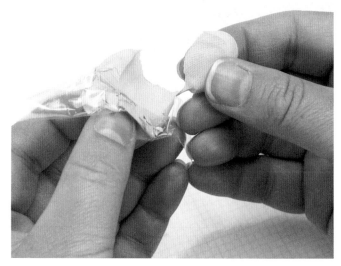

PREPARING TO WORK

Get your work space ready by having all of your basic tools at hand. Placing them within reach of your work surface saves you from having to look for an item once you get started. If you are using a mug warmer to dry metal clay, make sure you have it plugged into a nearby electric outlet.

Handling Clay

Metal clay is slightly sticky, so before handling it, lightly coat your hands with olive oil or a beeswax balm. After your hands are lubricated, wipe them across your work surface and roller to lubricate them well. Once your hands and work surface are ready, remove the clay from the package. Try not to get much more clay than you'll need for the project you are working on because metal clay can dry out quickly and become difficult to work with. Seal the remaining clay in the original package. While you are working on a project, make sure to keep any clay pieces you are not using under plastic wrap or a humidifier cup until you need them. This will help keep the clay moist.

Clay that needs further rolling to reintegrate all of the pieces

Using Scrap Clay

Clay fresh out of the package does not need any conditioning. However, if you use scraps from previous projects, you will need to firmly press and roll the clay scraps between your palms to reintegrate the clay scraps into one solid piece with no cracks or air pockets. If you can see the separate pieces of clay used to make up the new ball of clay, the pieces have not been pressed together firmly enough. Continue to roll the clay, pressing it firmly between your palms, until it becomes one smooth sphere.

Reintegrated clay

rolling clay

The starting point for most metal clay projects, including many of those in this book, is to roll out sheets of metal clay. By varying the number of playing cards supporting the roller on each side of the clay, you can determine the thickness of each metal clay sheet. I recommend making sets of taped card stacks to have ready for use. Make sure to label each taped stack so that you can easily tell how thick each stack is!

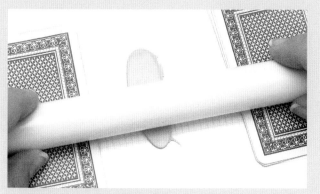

1. BEGIN ROLLING OUT CLAY

Place the clay on the work surface. Lay the desired number of cards on both sides of the clay to determine the final thickness of the clay sheet. Rub your lubricated hands over the roller to lubricate it. Lightly press the roller down on the clay and roll once over the clay.

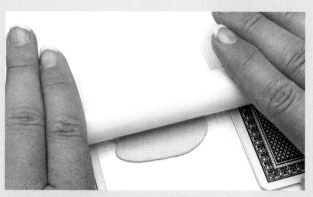

2. FINISH ROLLING OUT CLAY

Rotate the clay 90 degrees on the work surface. Roll firmly over the clay, pressing down so that the roller makes contact with the cards on both sides of the clay. If you need a long strip of clay, don't rotate the clay. Continue rolling in the same direction for each roll, and the clay will stay in a strip instead of spreading out.

CREATING & USING MOLDS

With the use of molds and metal clay comes an exciting possibility of duplicating three-dimensional objects in silver. By using a mold you can create a piece to use as a focal point or as an additional design element for your project. Commercial molds come in an array of shapes, sizes and designs. If you would rather make your work a little more distinctive, or if you would like to duplicate a specific object, you can make your own molds out of two-part molding compound or a less costly material, like polymer clay.

Creating a Polymer Clay Mold

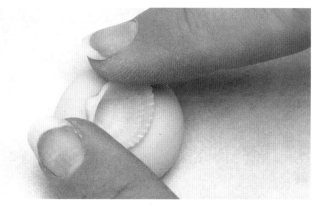

1. PRESS ITEM INTO POLYMER CLAY

Condition enough polymer clay to completely surround the item you wish to mold. Shape the polymer clay into a ball slightly larger than the object of your choice (here, a seashell). Brush a light coating of cornstarch or water onto the item you are molding so that it will come out of the polymer clay easily. Firmly press the object into the polymer clay.

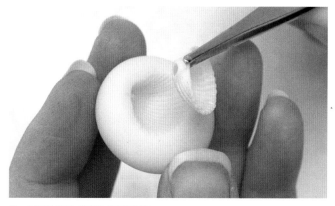

2. COMPLETE MOLD

Gently remove the object from the polymer clay, being careful not to distort the mold. Tweezers can be helpful in removing items from the polymer clay. Inspect the mold to make sure that all of the details have been impressed into the polymer clay. If you are satisfied with your mold, bake it according to the instructions printed on the polymer clay package.

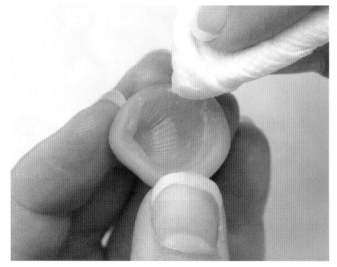

1. PREPARE MOLD

Thoroughly coat the mold with a thin layer of olive oil or balm. Make sure to work the lubricant into all of the details of the mold, or the metal clay may stick.

2. FILL MOLD WITH METAL CLAY

Shape the metal clay to roughly the size of the mold. Firmly press the metal clay into the mold. Work your fingers over the metal clay, pushing it into every detail of the mold. If you have trouble working the metal clay into the mold, try turning the mold open side down on the work surface and pushing the mold down onto the metal clay.

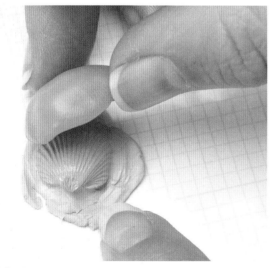

3. UNMOLD METAL CLAY

Once you have pushed the metal clay into the mold, turn the mold open side down on the work surface, hold down the lip of the excess clay with your finger and gently roll the mold off of the metal clay.

4. TRIM METAL CLAY

Cut the excess metal clay away from the molded metal clay with a craft knife or a needle tool.

ADDING TEXTURE TO CLAY

Adding texture to any project is a perfect way to add your own unique touch, as well as visual interest. Texture can be big and bold or small and subtle. Have fun and be creative with the textures you choose.

Texturing Clay

Rubber stamps are widely used for texturing metal clay, and they are available in seemingly limitless designs. When using rubber stamps, begin by applying balm or olive oil to the stamp. Roll out the metal clay (I suggest a five-card thickness when stamping clay), then press the stamp into the clay evenly. You can also gently roll over the stamp with a roller to make a deeper impression. If the clay sticks to the stamp when you are removing it, use a needle tool to gently pull the clay away from the stamp.

If you wish to expand your horizons beyond commercial products, try using some of the other items suggested on page 12. Be sure to lightly coat any object with olive oil or balm so the metal clay will not stick to the object. One of my favorite natural textures to use comes from a leaf. You can impress a leaf, vein side down, into a sheet of clay to get a beautiful silver leaf imprint.

However you choose to texture metal clay, pay close attention to the depth of the texture impression. Make sure you do not press farther down than half of the thickness of the clay sheet. Impressions that are more than half the thickness of the clay may thin out the sheet enough that you run the risk of holes forming in the clay during the firing process.

CUTTING CLAY PIECES

When it comes to cutting clay, you can choose from several methods. My favorite tools for cutting are my needle tool, tissue blade and craft knife. To make cutting shapes quick and easy, the polymer clay world gave birth to cutters in various shapes and sizes; these can also be used for metal clay. Drinking straws and stir straws make great circle cutters, and you can easily find different sizes at your favorite restaurants. You can also make your own templates for cutting clay out of paper, cardstock or thin cardboard, or you can purchase commercial templates in a variety of shapes and sizes.

Cutting Straight Lines

I find it easiest to cut straight lines using a tissue blade. If you use a template with straight edges, place the blade on the clay along the side of the template and press downward firmly, until the blade completely passes through the clay. If you cut straight lines freehand, you can use the lines on graph paper to make sure you make straight, parallel cuts.

Cutting Curved Lines

I prefer to use a needle tool to cut curved lines, whether I am following a template or cutting freehand. When you cut with a craft knife, you have to pay attention to the direction the blade is facing. With a needle tool, however, you can cut in any direction without having to rotate or change your grip on the needle tool.

Keeping Clay Scraps

The excess clay you cut away from a project piece can be used later, but metal clay dries out quickly and becomes difficult to work with. To keep metal clay scraps moist until you are ready to work with them, set up a humidifier cup. Mist the inside of a small plastic cup with water and place it over the clay scraps on the work surface. Put a weight, such as a balm container, on top of the plastic cup, and brush a line of water around the rim of the cup to seal in moisture.

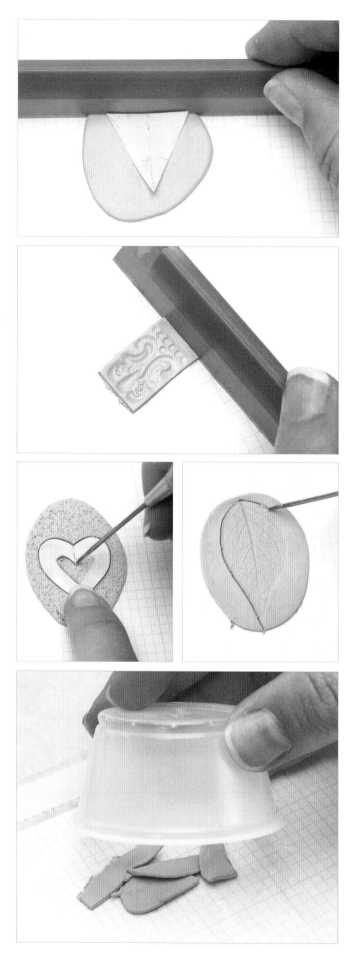

JOINING CLAY ELEMENTS

Properly attaching metal clay pieces to each other is important to the strength of a finished project. The clay pieces to be joined must be moist enough to activate the binder that will hold the pieces together during firing. Use paste and slip, which are both composed of metal clay thinned with water, to join pieces of metal clay together. The type of join you want to make will determine the thickness of the paste or slip you use.

Making Clay Paste

Metal clay paste is like glue for metal clay. Premixed paste is available from metal clay manufacturers, in the perfect consistency for making strong joins, such as those needed for attaching pendant bails, filling cracks and joining pieces with a small surface area. Paste adds bulk to a finished piece, but it can be thinned with water for less bulk (and a weaker join). If you do not have premixed paste on hand, you can make your own using a small piece of lump clay, a palette knife and a little distilled water, as shown below.

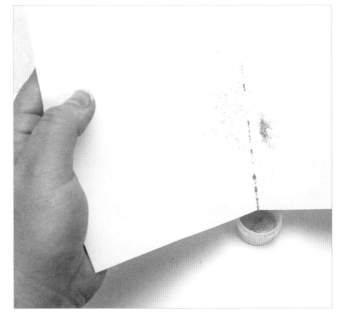

Making Clay Slip

Slip is a watered-down version of paste. I use slip to join leather-hard pieces of clay together and to smooth out rough areas before drying the clay. Brush slip over already attached small elements to help secure them to a piece.

I like to make slip by recycling the dried clay I sand off while refining my pieces. I collect all the metal clay powder, dump it into a small airtight container, then add water and a drop of vinegar (to inhibit mold). Occasionally, the slip has to be mixed with a palette knife to compress the binder and silver particles together. Over time, the slip will start to dry out as the water evaporates. When this happens, just spritz the slip with a bit of distilled water until you get the desired consistency.

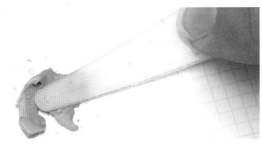

1. SPREAD CLAY
Using a palette knife, spread out a pea-size piece of clay on the work surface.

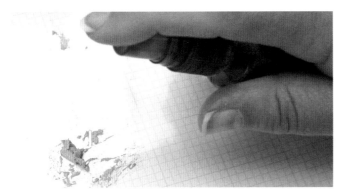

2. ADD WATER
Spray the clay with a small amount of distilled water.

3. MIX CLAY
Mix the water into the clay by firmly pressing the water into the clay with the palette knife. Continue to add water and mix until the clay paste reaches a toothpaste consistency.

LAYERING PIECES OF CLAY

When layering pieces of metal clay, you must use water, slip or paste. When metal clay is still moist, you can easily join pieces by brushing water on both connecting sides and pressing the pieces together. When the clay becomes leather hard or bone dry, use paste or slip between the joining pieces to make sure they attach with a strong bond.

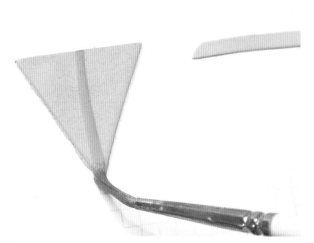

1. PREPARE BASE

Roll, texture and cut your metal clay pieces. Use a small paintbrush to apply a layer of water, slip or paste to the areas of the base that will be joined to other pieces.

2. PREPARE ADDITIONS

Apply a thin layer of slip or paste to the metal clay elements to be added to the base.

3. JOIN PIECES AND TRIM

Lay the metal clay additions on the base and press lightly to join the pieces together. Trim as needed.

4. SEAL EDGES

Once all of the clay elements are assembled, brush a line of water or slip along each seam where the pieces of clay are joined. If the pieces of clay being joined are small or irregular, you can also brush a light coat of water or slip over the entire surface of the piece to ensure that all of the joins are sealed. After the pieces are dried and refined, check for cracks or gaps in the joins. Fill any imperfections with slip or paste.

joining clay to form cylinders

Metal clay cylinders can be a focal point in a design or they can be beautiful beads. Making cylinders or tubes is a simple process. The keys to creating a beautiful cylinder are building around a cylindrical form and making a strong join. Use a thick paste to join the ends of a clay strip together. When you form a cylinder, use plenty of paste at the seam; you can always sand off any excess or texture the join to blend with the rest of the cylinder.

1. MEASURE CLAY
Roll, texture and cut clay to the desired size. Clay cylinders need support while they dry, so choose or make a tube or cylinder to support your clay. Here, I am using a drinking straw. Lightly coat the supportive tube with olive oil or balm. Roll the clay around the supportive tube. Cut the clay so that the ends of the strip will touch but not overlap.

2. JOIN ENDS
Apply a line of paste to each end of the clay strip and gently push the two ends together. Hold the ends together until they dry enough to hold the cylindrical shape. Allow the clay to dry until the cylinder looks bone dry on the outside. Then slide the clay cylinder off of the support to allow the inside of the clay cylinder to dry.

3. REFINE JOIN
Once the clay is completely dry, sand down any excess clay or paste around the join. If there are any cracks or gaps, reapply paste to the join and let it dry. Sand and inspect the join. Repeat pasting, drying and sanding until the join matches the rest of the cylinder. If you texturized the clay before joining it into a cylinder, apply a thin layer of paste over the join, allow it to dry for a few seconds and texture the area over the join.

CREATING BEZELS

A bezel is a type of setting normally used to secure a gemstone. A bezel surrounds the gemstone and holds it in place. Creating a bezel will seem familiar because it begins with the creation of a short cylinder, which is then joined to a base.

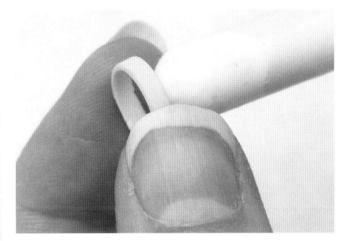

1. FORM CYLINDER
Roll and cut metal clay into a strip whose width is the desired height of your bezel. Follow Steps 1 through 3 at left to form a cylinder. You can also form bezels in shapes other than circles by forming a support out of polymer clay (see *Tantalizing Teardrop Necklace*, on page 92).

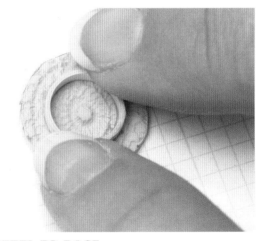

2. JOIN BEZEL TO BASE
Roll, texture and cut metal clay to your base dimensions. Apply a line of water or slip on the base where the bezel is to be placed, and apply water on the bottom edge of the dried bezel. Gently press the bezel into the base, approximately halfway through the base's clay. Brush water around the inside and outside edges of the bezel where it meets the base.

CREATING RINGS

Although making rings may seem a bit tricky, you can perfect this procedure by paying close attention to how and where you measure for the ring. The type of ring you choose to make is also important. An open-wrap ring can be adjusted if the ring does not come out exactly the size you anticipated, but extra care must be taken when creating a solid-cylinder ring. Remember: Measure twice, cut once.

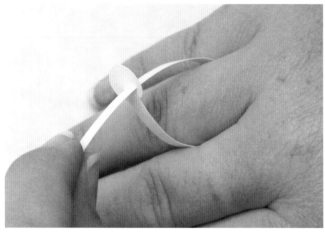

1. CREATE RING SIZER
Using the template on page 126, create a ring sizer from thick paper or cardstock. Place the tip of the ring sizer through the slit in the round end. Place the ring sizer on the finger you are measuring.

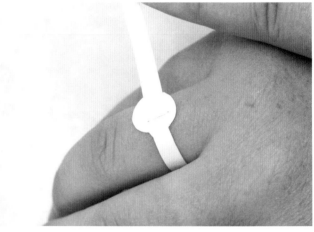

2. MEASURE FINGER
Find the thickest part of the finger (usually at the base or knuckle) and tighten the ring sizer there until it is snug but not tight. Bend back the end of the ring sizer to mark the ring size. Remove the ring sizer from the finger and measure the length in millimeters from the bend you made in the ring sizer to the slit in the round end. This should be the circumference of the ring after firing.

3. CREATE RING FORM
To account for the 12 percent shrinkage of metal clay, divide your ring circumference found in Step 2 by 88 percent. For example, if you want a ring with a 65mm circumference, form from metal clay a ring that measures 74mm before firing (65mm ÷ 88 percent = 74mm). When the ring is fired it will shrink to 88 percent of its unfired size (74mm × 88 percent = 65mm). Once you determine the unfired circumference of the ring, set the ring sizer to that length. Tightly roll a sheet of light cardstock, place it inside the ring sizer and let it expand to fill the ring sizer. Tape the cardstock to maintain the proper size.

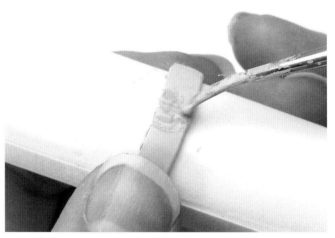

4. JOIN CLAY INTO RING
Roll, texture and cut clay to the desired width and length equal to the unfired circumference from Step 3. Follow Steps 1 through 3 of *Joining Clay to Form Cylinders* (see page 25) to form a ring, using the ring form to support the clay as it dries. Add embellishments as desired.

CREATING BAILS

In most cases, to have a nicely formed pendant, you should design the piece with a bail for stringing. Bails are generally more aesthetically pleasing than just a hole poked in the top of a pendant. A bail can be a totally separate piece of clay attached to the pendant, or the bail can be incorporated as part of the pendant design. Below are a few of my favorite quick and easy bail styles.

Creating a Tube Bail with a Tail

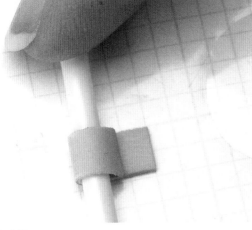

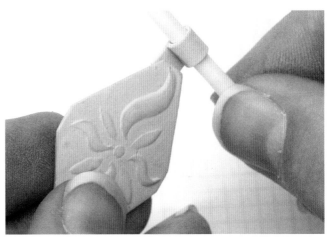

1. FORM BAIL

Roll, texture and cut a strip of clay. Roll the clay strip around a lubricated support tube (here, a thin straw) until the end of the strip touches the clay tail. Do not cut the clay tail. Use paste to join the end of the clay strip to the remaining tail, forming a P shape. Allow the bail to dry on the support tube.

2. ATTACH BAIL TO PENDANT

Join the tail of the bail to the pendant body (see *Layering Pieces of Clay*, page 24).

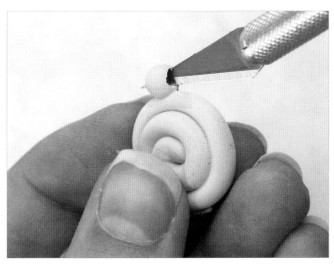

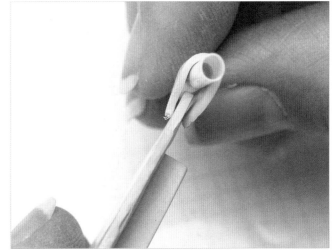

Creating a Ball Bail

To form a ball bail, first join a ball of clay to the pendant body (see *Layering Pieces of Clay*, page 24). After the clay has dried, drill a hole in the ball of clay (see *Creating Holes in Dry Clay*, page 28).

Creating a Sandwich Bail

Add a sandwich bail to a pendant by joining the ends of a strip of clay to both the front and back of a pendant, sandwiching the pendant (see *Layering Pieces of Clay*, page 24).

MAKING HOLES IN CLAY

Creating holes in metal clay plays an important role in many designs. Some projects need holes for stringing or assembly; others use them as design elements.

Creating Holes in Wet Clay

To create holes in wet clay, use a toothpick or needle tool. For larger holes, a lightly oiled straw can be used to punch out holes, or a needle tool can be used to cut holes freehand. After the clay dries, be sure to use a craft knife or sandpaper to refine the inside edges of any holes you created while the clay was wet.

If you forget to make holes in your clay before firing, you can drill holes in the fired piece with a drill bit.

Creating Holes in Dry Clay

I find it easiest to create a hole in dried clay using a small drill bit. The tip of a craft knife can also be used to create holes. Simply position it on the clay and rotate it, using the tip as a drill to work through the clay.

A hole should be at least as far from the edge as the hole is wide. For example, if you make a 2mm-diameter hole, it should not be any closer than 2mm from the edge. For this reason, I prefer to create holes in the clay after it has been refined. Once a piece is refined, I know exactly where the edges are, and I can accurately place the holes.

DRYING CLAY

Before you refine and fire metal clay, the clay must be bone dry so it will be strong enough to withstand sanding and drilling. Thoroughly drying clay before firing it is also important because firing moist clay can cause blisters and cracks in the finished piece, weakening it and marring its appearance. Metal clay will dry completely at room temperature in eight to twelve hours, depending on humidity, the type of clay used and the thickness of the clay.

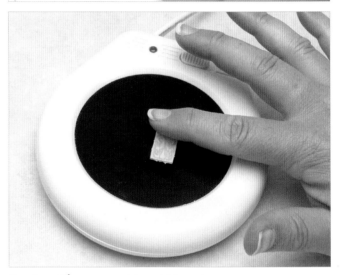

Drying Clay on a Mug Warmer

To speed up the drying process, I use a mug warmer. When you are ready to dry the clay, place it on a mug warmer and gently pat the clay flat. The heat causes the water in the clay to evaporate in a matter of minutes. Handle the clay carefully when removing it from the mug warmer, as the clay will be hot.

If you dry a cylinder or ring, begin drying the piece on its support item, such as a straw or dowel. Once the clay looks bone dry on the outside of the cylinder, remove the support item to allow the clay on the interior of the cylinder to dry.

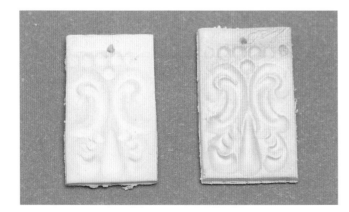

REFINING DRY CLAY

Once your piece is bone dry, sand and refine any rough or uneven areas. Cracks, sharp edges and rough spots present before firing will still be there afterward. The refining stage is a good time to check joins, edges and bails: Look for secure attachments and repair any unwanted holes or gaps. Remember that the dried clay is fragile before firing, so hold the piece firmly and sand it gently. For extra support, hold the piece close to the edge when sanding.

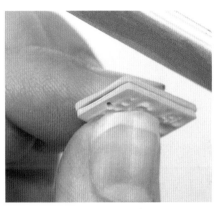

1. REFINE OUTER EDGES

Use a nail file or sandpaper to smooth the edges and corners of dried clay pieces. If you need to remove large amounts of clay, start with a medium or coarse grit, such as 200. For removing small amounts of clay, use a fine grit, such as 1,000. As the clay is fired it will shrink and corners can become sharp, so make sure to slightly round corners or points so the finished jewelry is comfortable to wear.

2. REFINE INNER EDGES

The inner edges of any openings in the clay should also be refined. A rolled-up piece of sandpaper or needle file works in most openings. A needle file or the tip of a craft knife can be used to smooth any spaces too small for sandpaper.

3. COMPARE PIECES (OPTIONAL)

If you are making two or more matching pieces, such as earrings, compare all of the pieces to ensure they are the same size. If they aren't, hold the pieces back-to-back and sand the larger piece until it matches the smaller one.

4. MARK WORK (OPTIONAL)

I highly recommend marking all of your work. Use a needle tool to mark your initials and the contents of your piece (.999FS for silver metal clay) on the back of your work.

breaks and repairs

Dried metal clay is fragile. If a piece breaks, you can usually mend it using paste. Repairing a break is similar to joining pieces of wet clay together. Brush a line of water on each area that will be joined together, wait about ten seconds, then brush a generous amount of slip or paste onto the same areas. Press the pieces together and hold them in place for a few seconds while the slip starts to dry, or place the joined pieces on a flat surface so they will have even support. If there is slip or paste oozing from the join, smooth it out with a blending tool or a damp paintbrush. Dry and refine the piece as usual, then inspect the repair. Repeat the repair steps until the break is no longer noticeable.

FIRING

During the firing process, the organic binder in the metal clay burns off and the metal particles sinter, or fuse together. To achieve this, the metal clay must be brought to sintering temperature and then held there until the metal particles fuse. See the firing chart on page 14 for the firing time a piece will need. You can use several methods to fire metal clay. The most cost-effective method is a handheld butane torch, which can fire objects that weigh up to 25 grams.

Follow the manufacturer's instructions before using any type of firing device. Any firing device could pose a hazard if not properly operated. Fire only on an approved firing surface in a well-ventilated area. Wear safety glasses and leather gloves, and secure long hair and any loose clothing. Do not leave any operating firing device unattended, and do not operate firing devices around children or pets.

Firing Metal Clay with a Torch

Place a bone-dry clay piece on a firing surface. Begin to warm the piece by slowly moving the torch flame around the piece's edges. Work your way toward the center, slowly moving the torch in circles. Make sure to always keep the flame moving and to heat the entire surface of the piece. The clay may darken, give off wisps of smoke and catch fire as the binder in the clay burns off. The larger the piece, the more likely it is to exhibit smoke and flames.

Continue to move the flame over the piece until it glows a soft orange. Once it has reached this cantaloupe color, hold the piece at this stage for the amount of time indicated in the firing chart on page 14. Always keep the torch flame moving over the piece, heating the entire surface evenly, as the particles bond together.

If the piece begins to glow a brighter orange, slowly pull the flame back until the piece fades back to the cantaloupe color. A brighter orange indicates that the metal is getting too hot and could melt.

Once you have maintained fusing temperature for the amount of time required, turn off the torch and allow the metal to cool, or carefully quench the metal in a container of water. Be very careful with the newly fired metal, as it will be extremely hot. Use tweezers or tongs to handle it until the piece has cooled completely.

Overheating

It is possible to overheat or even melt metal clay if you do not keep your torch flame moving. If you heat the clay too much, it will progress from pale orange to a bright, glowing orange. If you heat it further, it will begin to shimmer and have a liquid shine like that of mercury. This means the metal is melting and may lose its shape.

If you notice your piece turning bright orange, slowly pull the flame back from the piece until the soft orange glow resumes.

On the left: a properly fired piece of clay. On the right: a piece that was overheated on the right-hand side, resulting in a mercury-like appearance.

The small flames coming from this molded piece indicate that the binder in the metal clay is burning off.

The cantaloupe color of this piece indicates that the metal clay has reached fusing temperature.

BURNISHING

By burnishing a piece of fired metal clay, you compress the metal particles to reflect light. When you have fired a clay piece and it has cooled completely, you will see that it has a white finish. This is because the sintered metal is porous and needs to be burnished. The first step in this process is to brass brush your piece with a little soap and water for lubrication. If you want a shinier finish, the second step is to compress or rub the piece with a tool, such as a stainless steel or agate burnisher. If you do not have those items handy, burnishing with a stainless steel spoon will give the piece a nice finish. If you prefer a high-polished mirror finish, you will need to invest in a tumbler with stainless steel shot.

Spoon Burnishing

To acheive a higher shine, after brush burnishing rub the piece firmly with the back of a stainless steel spoon. The increased pressure will help to further compress the metal particles, resulting in a shinier finish. This can also be done with stainless steel or agate burnishers.

Brush Burnishing

1. BEGIN BURNISHING
After the metal has completely cooled, wet the piece with soapy water. Use a soft brass brush to burnish down the metal particles.

2. COMPLETE BURNISHING
Continue to vigorously brush the metal until the entire piece has a satin finish.

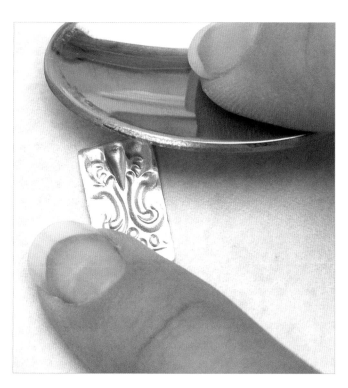

ADDING COLOR OR PATINA

After it is fired and burnished, metal clay jewelry is ready to wear. If you want to take your creations even further, you can use these treatments to brighten up pieces with color or to make them smoky and sultry with a patina. A patina on a highly textured silver piece will bring out the design by darkening the crevices. Adding color to your designs can make them vibrant and add visual interest. Try these techniques to see just how far you can push your creativity.

Adding Colored Two-Part Epoxy

Adding colored two-part epoxy to a fired piece is a quick and easy way to beautify your work. For small projects, I prefer a quick-setting adhesive epoxy for attaching and coloring pieces. To color the epoxy resin, you can mix it with mica powders, oil paints, metallic paints or inks. Epoxy does have an odor, so make sure to work in a well-ventilated area.

adding oil paint

This is what I like to call "Patina in a Pinch," a faux patina method. This is a great way to darken a piece without dealing with mixing chemicals. Black oil paint is easy to obtain and much quicker to use than chemical patinas. You can also try different colors of oil paint for a completely new look!

1. MIX EPOXY
Mix the two-part epoxy according to the manufacturer's instructions. Use a toothpick to thoroughly mix your colorant of choice into the epoxy. Here, I am using mica powder.

1. APPLY PAINT
Using your finger, apply oil paint to the surface you wish to patinate. Rub the oil paint into all of the crevices on the surface of the piece.

2. REMOVE EXCESS PAINT
While the paint is still wet, buff off the excess with a paper towel. Rub lightly so you remove only the paint from the surface of the piece and not from the crevices.

2. APPLY EPOXY
With a toothpick, add epoxy to the metal surface. If there are any bubbles trapped in the epoxy, gently tap the piece on a hard surface so that the bubbles will rise to the surface, where you can pop them with a needle. Before the epoxy dries, use a clean toothpick to remove any excess.

Using Liver of Sulfur

Liver of sulfur is available in liquid or solid form and it must be stored in an airtight, lightproof container. I recommend using the solid form because it comes in small pieces that can be mixed with water to form a solution at your convenience. Although liver of sulfur has a nasty smell (think rotten eggs), it is very useful in the enhancement of metal clay objects. But this is not an exact science. Dipping your metal clay pieces in a liver of sulfur solution can produce a rainbow of colors from golden yellow to blue-black and everything in between.

The colors are unpredictable, but the result is usually a happy surprise. To aid in getting a variety of colors, add a bit of ammonia to the dipping mixture. If you want to add a patina to a pair of earrings, I suggest stringing them together and dipping both at the same time so that you will obtain similar results on each. If you like the results, coat the piece with Renaissance Wax or a good spray lacquer to protect the surface. If you are not happy with the colors, you can remove the patina by heating the metal with a torch.

1. PREPARE MIXTURE

Dissolve a pea-size piece of liver of sulfur in 1 cup (237ml) of warm water. Place the container on a mug warmer to keep it warm. Dissolve 1 teaspoon (5ml) of baking soda in 1 cup (237ml) of cold water. Thoroughly clean the fired and burnished metal piece. Handle the piece with tweezers so that you do not get any skin oils on the surface of the piece; such oils may cause an irregular patina.

2. SOAK METAL

Holding the metal clay piece with tweezers, heat the piece with hot water, then place the piece in the liver of sulfur mixture. The longer the metal is in the mixture, the darker it will become. When the metal reaches the shade you desire, remove the piece from the liver of sulfur solution using tweezers.

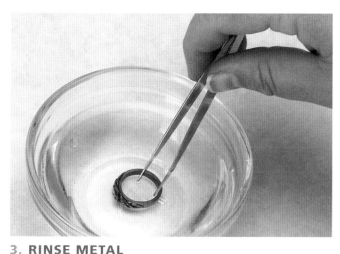

3. RINSE METAL

Swish the metal piece around in the baking soda mixture for 5 to 10 seconds to stop the patination process. Remove the piece, and dry it thoroughly.

4. POLISH RAISED AREAS (OPTIONAL)

Use a silver polishing cloth or a jeweler's pad to remove the patina from any areas you wish to remain bright.

Making Jewelry

MATERIALS

Now that you have this striking piece of silver you may be wondering what to do with it. Decisions, decisions. Sometimes it will take some thought to come up with a plan for your project, and other times you will know exactly what you need to do to make a fabulous, one-of-a-kind piece of art jewelry. Well, to make your piece into wearable art you will need a few tools and supplies. Have fun playing with the wide variety of beads, findings and tools available to create your own beautiful jewelry.

BASIC JEWELRY TOOL KIT

When it comes to assembling jewelry, sometimes the look of the finished piece can depend on the type of tools used. Half the battle in creating beautiful jewelry is having the right tools (the other half is using them properly; see *Techniques*, pages 36–37). Listed below are a few tools that I find invaluable for jewelry assembly. You can find these at craft, jewelry and beading stores, and even some home improvement stores.

Round-nose pliers are used to make loops in wire. Round-nose pliers have tapered tips, so you can make a range of loop sizes.

Chain-nose pliers are used to grasp, hold, bend and form wire. These flat-jawed pliers taper to a point, so they are great for getting into small places to make clean wire bends and tightly wrapped loops.

Wire cutters are a must-have tool for cutting wire, beading wire, eye pins and head pins. Although you do not need to buy the most expensive pair on the market, I suggest finding a good-quality pair; you will use these quite frequently, and the cheap ones usually do not hold up well.

Crimping pliers are used to curl and then flatten crimp tubes, used at the end of a string of beads to connect a clasp.

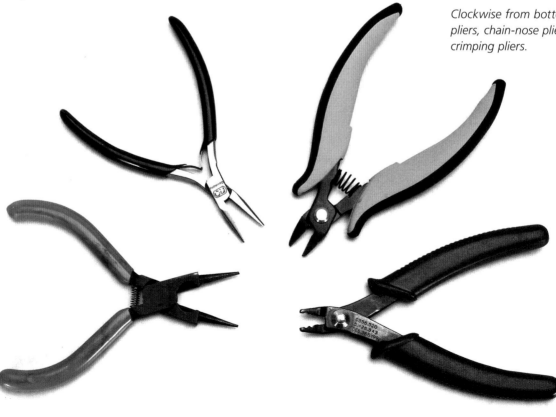

Clockwise from bottom left: round-nose pliers, chain-nose pliers, wire cutters, and crimping pliers.

JEWELRY SUPPLIES

Jewelry supplies known as findings are the key components to finishing wearable art jewelry. They are used for stringing, closing, connecting and decorating. Each of these items is used in the projects in this book and can be found in some variety stores and in craft, bead and jewelry supply stores.

Beading wire is a thin, flexible wire used to string beads, and it's available in various sizes and strand counts. Beading wire is composed of cabled steel strands with nylon coating. To add strength to your piece, use the thickest wire that will fit through the components.

Wire is available in many different materials, such as sterling silver, color-coated copper and niobium, and it can be used to hold jewelry together or as a decorative element. Wire is available in different thicknesses, or gauges. The thicker the wire, the stronger the connections in the jewelry.

Beads are great for adding colors and textures to metal clay jewelry. Available in every shape, size and composition you can imagine, you are sure to find beads to complement any metal clay piece. Beads are made from many different materials, including gemstones, semiprecious gems, glass, metal, wood, polymer clay and shell.

Pin backs can be glued or soldered to the back of a piece to convert it to a pin or brooch. Pin backs are available in a variety of sizes and styles. The larger the brooch or pin, the larger the pin back should be.

Jump rings are ideal for connecting clasps to bead strands. These rigid, tempered rings can be opened and closed using pliers. They are available in a wide selection of materials and sizes.

Head pins are pieces of straight wire that have a flat head on one end. These can be used to make bead dangles and to attach beads to loops. These are available in different lengths and materials, including silver, gold and base metals.

Eye pins are pieces of straight wire with a loop on the end for hanging and attaching to other jewelry components. These are available in different lengths and materials, including silver, gold and base metals.

Clockwise, from top left: beading wire, wire, pin backs, clasps, chain, ear wires and beads; center, from left: jump rings, head and eye pins and crimp tubes

Crimp tubes are used to connect bead-stringing material to a clasp. Crimp tubes are available in a variety of metals so that you can match them to other jewelry components.

Clasps are fasteners used to connect the ends of a necklace, bracelet or other piece of jewelry. Clasps come in a variety of forms, such as lobster claws, spring rings, box catches and toggles. They are also available in a wide variety of metals.

Ear wires are used to connect the earring body to the wearer's ear. Ear wires are available in a wide variety of materials to match the other earring components. To add a fun hint of color, I sometimes use colored niobium ear wires.

Chains can be used for hanging pendants, creating bracelets and stringing beads. Chains come in various sizes and shapes. I recommend using sterling silver chains with metal clay pieces.

TECHNIQUES

In order to finish your new creation, you need to know a few basic jewelry-making techniques. Although many techniques can be used to create custom-made jewelry, these basic techniques will help you begin creating necklaces, bracelets, earrings and other forms of wearable art. Properly using jewelry findings will make jewelry that is strong and long-lasting. For creating metal clay jewelry, I recommend using high-quality materials, such as sterling silver or gold-filled findings and wire. Using anything less would be like hanging fuzzy dice in a Mercedes—that's just not right.

OPENING & CLOSING JUMP RINGS

Jump rings have many uses, but their most important function is to connect jewelry components. Jump rings are available in assorted sizes and materials, so you should always be able to find the right one to meet your needs. (If you like working with wire, you can even make your own jump rings.) Using the proper technique to open and close jump rings is very important to the look and strength of finished jewelry; using the wrong technique will both weaken and misshape the jump rings. Make sure to practice this technique before you begin working on your own jewelry.

OPENING EAR WIRES & EYE PINS

Open the loop at the bottom of an ear wire or eye pin using the same method used to open a jump ring. Grasp the free end of the loop with pliers and twist it to the side. Add the jewelry components, then close the ear wire or eye pin by using pliers to twist the loop back into the closed position.

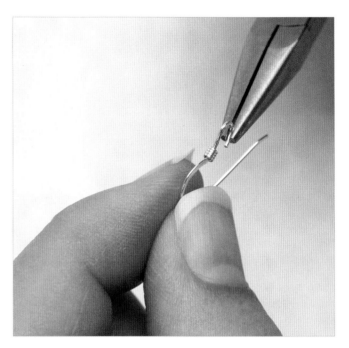

1. OPEN JUMP RING
Grasp the jump ring with pliers on both sides of the break. I like to use a pair of round-nose pliers and a pair of chain-nose pliers for this task. To open the ring, keep one pair of pliers stationary and rotate the other pair away from yourself.

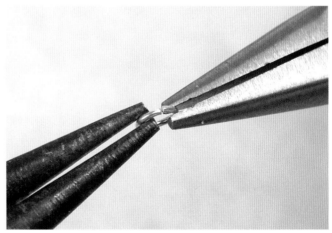

2. CLOSE JUMP RING
To close the jump ring, rotate the pliers in the opposite direction, moving the ends past each other, then back toward each other until they line up cleanly.

CREATING LOOPS IN HEAD PINS & EYE PINS

It is easy to connect jewelry components using head pins or eye pins. All you need is a pair of round-nose pliers to make a loop in the wire, a pair of wire cutters to cut off any excess and a pair of chain-nose pliers to tighten the loop. Practice making perfect loops using inexpensive base-metal wire before using sterling silver or gold-filled wire.

1. BEND WIRE
String component(s) onto a head pin or eye pin. Grasp the pin above the jewelry components with round-nose pliers and wrap the wire around the pliers, forming a loop.

2. CUT WIRE
Trim off the excess wire just before the point where the ends cross. Use chain-nose pliers to tighten the loop so that it is fully closed with no gaps.

crimping

Because crimp tubes are used to connect a clasp to a necklace or bracelet, they are very important to the structure of jewelry. Crimping properly ensures the strength of a finished piece. Make sure to use the proper tool, a set of crimping pliers, when you work with crimp tubes. Follow these steps to make a perfect crimp every time!

1. SLIDE WIRE THROUGH CLASP AND CRIMP TUBE
Cut a length of wire 2"-3" (5-8cm) longer than the finished length of the piece. Thread a crimp tube onto the wire, about 1" (3cm) from the end. Thread the end of the wire through the clasp and back through the crimp tube. Slide the crimp tube up to the clasp.

2. SECURE WIRES IN TUBE
Make sure that the wires are not crossed inside the crimp tube. Place the crimp tube into the bottom slot on the crimp tool and create an indention in the middle of the tube, securing the wires inside the tube.

3. FOLD CRIMP TUBE IN HALF
Move the indented crimp tube back to the first indention in the crimp tool and fold the tube in half.

EARRINGS
FOR EVERYONE

Earrings are thought to have originated in Asia and the Middle East. Both hoop and pendant earrings have been found in archeological digs that date back approximately 4,000 years. Pierced earrings date back to around 3,500 years ago in ancient Egypt. Earrings were always a sign of wealth and prosperity, as only the well-to-do women could afford the precious metals used to make earrings. Throughout the Dark and Middle Ages, most women were too poor to own earrings, and up until late in the Renaissance, earrings were looked upon as flashy and inappropriate for proper women. But today you see earrings everywhere, sometimes in places you do not want to see them (but I digress … that is a different topic).

Today earrings are fashionable, trendy, generally inexpensive, must-have accessories to complete a wardrobe, and both men and women of all ages wear them. You can find earrings in more shapes, styles and colors than you can shake a stick at. From simple studs and hoops for everyday wear to crystal-laden chandelier earrings you would only wear to a ball (or to play dress-up with your daughter or granddaughter), it is easy to find something for everyone these days. The great thing about being in this do-it-yourself era is having the ability and resources to make a pair of earrings to match that new outfit in about the same time it takes to get ready for a dinner party. With the introduction of metal clay to your craft box, you will be able to add fine silver to those earrings for a stunning, one-of-a-kind look.

Earrings are a great introductory metal clay project because they are small, quick to make and use little metal clay. A single 25 gram package of metal clay will yield several pairs of beautiful earrings. In this chapter you will discover a variety of ways to create beautiful earrings to suit any taste. From the whimsical *Heart Links in a Wink Earrings* (page 44) to the elegant *Resin with Reason Earrings* (page 52), you will find something to love in this chapter. The projects in this chapter are ordered according to difficulty. I suggest starting out with the simple but lovely *Flattering Flatware Earrings* (page 40) if you are new to metal clay. Throughout this chapter, I will show you techniques that you will carry with you throughout your metal clay journey. Once you have some experience under your belt, move on and experiment with a more advanced project, like the *Galactic Cylinder Earrings* (page 60). So jump right in and let me "bend your ear" about earrings!

These earrings are simple and classic. By using one of the most common utensils in your house, you can easily make earrings that look like you spent all day carving. A fun part of this project will be discovering just how many different designs you can come up with using various pieces of flatware. Have an old set of silverware you inherited from your great-grandmother? Now you can preserve that image in fine silver that you can wear. You do not have to limit yourself to the flatware in your kitchen drawer, either. Plastic flatware sometimes has wonderful design work, too. Start hunting for fabulous designs to turn into beautiful jewelry!

MATERIALS

4g low-fire metal clay

utensil with decorative handle

metal spoon

2 sterling silver ear wires

basic metal clay tool kit (see page 17)

basic jewelry tool kit (see page 34)

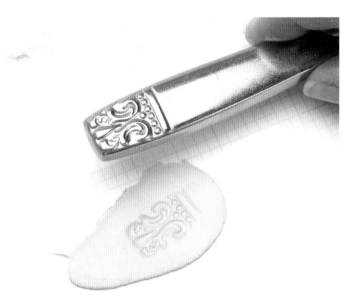

1. STAMP CLAY

Prepare your hands and work surface for working with metal clay (see *Handling Clay*, page 18). Roll metal clay to a five-card thickness (see *Rolling Clay*, page 19). Apply a light layer of olive oil or beeswax balm to the decorative handle of your chosen utensil. Lightly press the decorative handle into the clay; be careful not to thin the clay by pressing too hard. Hold the edge of the clay with your fingertip, and gently roll the utensil off of the clay.

2. CUT CLAY PIECES

Using a tissue blade, cut the clay so that the stamped design is centered on the clay. I cut these earrings to ½" × ¾" (1cm × 2cm).

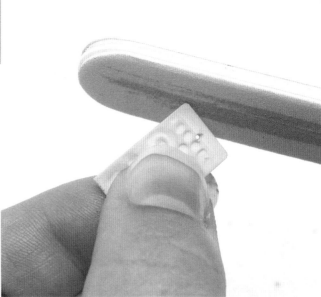

3. CREATE HOLE FOR EAR WIRE

Use a toothpick to make a hole for the ear wire at the top center of the piece (see *Creating Holes in Wet Clay*, page 28). If you are working on graph paper you can use the marked grid to help you find the center of the clay piece.

4. DRY AND REFINE CLAY

Allow the metal clay to dry completely. Once the clay is dry, refine the edges and round the corners slightly (see *Refining Dry Clay*, page 29). Use the tip of a craft knife to refine the toothpick hole.

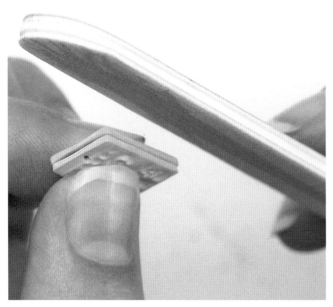

5. MATCH EARRING COMPONENTS

Repeat Steps 1 through 4 to make a second earring dangle. Compare the 2 metal clay pieces to ensure they are the same size. If the pieces are not the same size, file the larger piece until the two pieces match.

6. FIRE METAL CLAY

Individually fire each metal clay piece (see *Firing Metal Clay with a Torch*, page 30). Use the firing chart on page 14 to determine firing time.

7. BRUSH BURNISH METAL

Allow the metal to completely cool. Burnish each piece with a brass brush in soapy water (see *Brush Burnishing*, page 31).

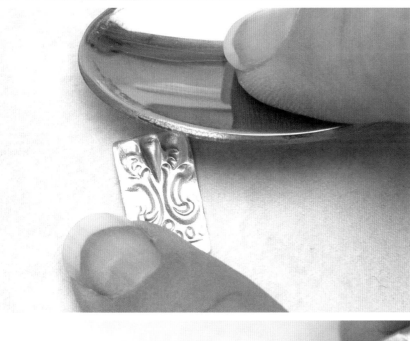

8. SPOON BURNISH METAL

Vigorously rub the surface of each piece with the back of a metal spoon until you are satisfied with the metal's sheen.

9. ASSEMBLE EARRING

Open the loop at the bottom of an ear wire, hook a metal clay piece onto the loop, and close the loop (see *Opening Ear Wires & Eye Pins*, page 36). Repeat for the second earring.

tip

If you are in a pinch for an ear wire, a jump ring or an eye pin, you can use wire to create your own.

I am sure you have heard the phrase "How do I love thee? Let me count the ways." Well, you can count on loving these heart earrings. The fun, feminine look of these connected heart dangles is easy to achieve. For this project, the clay gets textured and then cut into the heart pieces. After the firing process, a quick and easy faux finish completes the look. So whether you are young or just young at heart, these earrings are cute enough to wear anytime, and even more special around Valentine's Day.

MATERIALS

7g low-fire metal clay

nylon scrub pad

metal spoon

black oil paint

paper towel

2 sterling silver ear wires

2 sterling silver jump rings

basic metal clay tool kit (see page 17)

basic jewelry tool kit (see page 34)

1. TEXTURE CLAY

Prepare your hands and work surface for working with metal clay (see *Handling Clay*, page 18). Roll metal clay to a four-card thickness (see *Rolling Clay*, page 19). Dab the rolled metal clay with a nylon scrub pad for texture.

2. CUT CLAY

Use the heart template for this project on page 126 to cut the earring components (see *Cutting Curved Lines*, page 22).

45

3. SEPARATE COMPONENTS

Remove the outer scrap clay, then separate the large heart from the small heart. Make sure to handle the clay carefully, as you will use both hearts in the earrings.

4. CREATE HOLES FOR ASSEMBLY

Use a toothpick to make a hole for the ear wire at the top center of the large heart (see *Creating Holes in Wet Clay*, page 28). Make additional holes for joining the two hearts: 1 hole at the bottom of the large heart and 1 hole on the side of the small heart.

5. REFINE COMPONENTS

Allow the metal clay components to dry completely. Refine the inside and outside edges of each clay piece (see *Refining Dry Clay*, page 29). Use the tip of a craft knife to refine the toothpick holes in the clay pieces. Repeat Steps 1 through 5 to create components for the second earring. Compare the like components to ensure they are the same size. If the like components do not match, file the larger piece to match the smaller piece.

6. APPLY OIL PAINT FOR FAUX FINISH

Fire each heart individually, following the firing chart on page 14 (see *Firing Metal Clay with a Torch*, page 30). Burnish each dangle, first with a soft brass brush, then with the back of a metal spoon (see *Burnishing*, page 31). Apply black oil paint to the surface of each piece. Rub the oil paint firmly into all of the crevices you created with the nylon scrub pad.

7. BUFF OFF EXCESS PAINT

While the paint is still wet, buff off the excess with a paper towel. Rub lightly, so you only remove the paint from the surface of the piece and not from the crevices.

8. ASSEMBLE EARRINGS

Connect a large heart component to a small heart dangle with a jump ring (see *Opening and Closing Jump Rings*, page 36). Open the loop at the bottom of an ear wire, hook the large heart onto the loop and close the loop (see *Opening Ear Wires and Eye Pins*, page 36). Repeat for the second earring.

tip

To ensure you will have slip or paste ready when you need it, make some ahead of time and keep it on hand. Old 35mm film canisters are great airtight storage containers for slip and paste.

With these earrings, you will look at geometry in a whole new light. These eye-catching triangular dangles incorporate three different surface patterns for a complex look that is easy to achieve. A smooth strip of clay divides two contrasting textures, created using only a pencil and a craft knife. With this project, you will also learn how to layer clay, adding new dimensions to your work. For a touch of color, a lovely triangular bead tops off each earring. Go ahead, take a chance and "tri" these earrings!

MATERIALS

6g low-fire metal clay

metal clay slip or paste

pencil

metal spoon

2 sterling silver ear wires

2 sterling silver eye pins

2 8mm × 6mm aqua flower cone beads

basic metal clay tool kit (see page 17)

basic jewelry tool kit (see page 34)

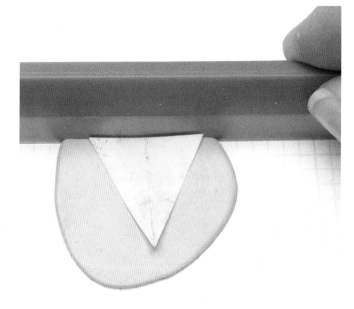

1. CUT TRIANGLE
Prepare your hands and work surface for working with metal clay (see *Handling Clay*, page 18). Roll metal clay to a four-card thickness (see *Rolling Clay*, page 19). Cut the metal clay using the triangle template for this project on page 126 (see *Cutting Straight Lines*, page 22).

2. CUT CLAY STRIP
Roll the remaining metal clay to a two-card thickness. Cut a ⅛" × 2" (3mm × 5cm) strip of clay.

49

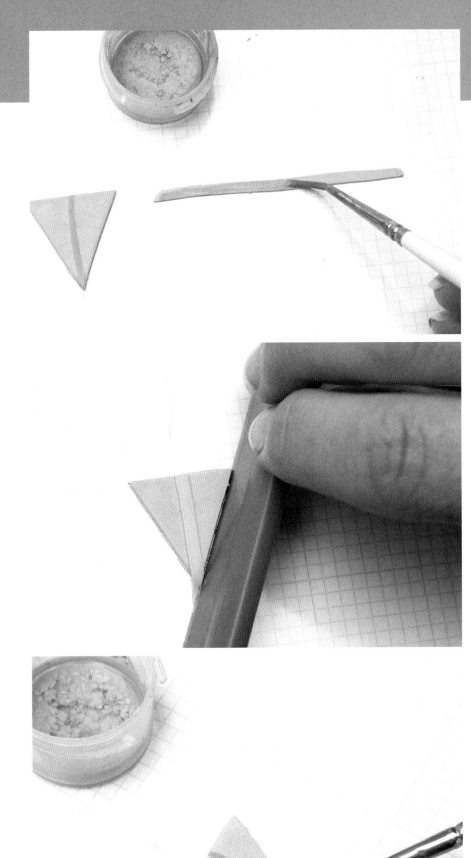

3. JOIN PIECES

Brush a line of slip down the center of the triangle and onto the back of the clay strip. Join the clay strip to the triangle (see *Layering Pieces of Clay*, page 24).

4. TRIM CLAY

Using a tissue blade, cut the clay strip along the top and point of the triangle.

5. SEAL JOINS

Seal the clay strip to the triangle by brushing slip along the edges where the two pieces meet.

6. INDENT CLAY

Using the tip of a pencil, make several indentations in the clay triangle to one side of the clay strip. Don't press more than halfway through the thickness of the metal clay. Allow the clay to dry completely.

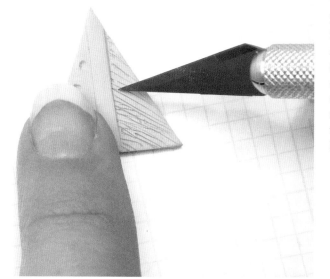

7. SCRATCH CLAY

Scratch the smooth half of the triangle with the tip of a craft knife. Smooth and refine all of the edges of the metal clay (see *Refining Dry Clay*, page 29). Create a hole at the top of the earring with a small drill bit or the tip of a craft knife (see *Creating Holes in Dry Clay*, page 28). Repeat Steps 1 through 7 to create a second earring component. Mirror the placement of the indentations and scratches on the second piece. Compare the triangles to ensure they are the same size. If the triangles do not match, file the larger to match the smaller.

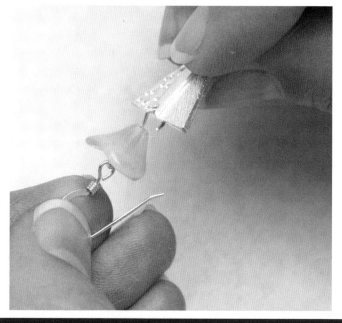

8. ASSEMBLE EARRING

Fire each piece of metal clay individually following the firing chart on page 14 (see *Firing Metal Clay with a Torch*, page 30). Allow both pieces to cool completely. Burnish each piece, first with a soft brass brush, then with the back of a metal spoon (see *Burnishing*, page 31). Slide a flower cone bead onto an eye pin and close the open end of the eye pin with a loop (see *Creating Loops in Head Pins and Eye Pins* on page 37). Open the loop at the top of the eye pin, hook an ear wire onto the loop, and close the loop (see *Opening Ear Wires and Eye Pins*, page 36). Open the loop at the bottom of the eye pin, hook a triangle onto the loop and close. Repeat for the second earring.

Simply put, I love color. I also love the look of enamel, but glass enamel can be challenging to work with. This elegant pair of marquise-shaped earrings allows you to have the look of enamel with less cost, less time and without the painstaking process of working with glass enamel. To create these earrings, layer metal clay to form a well, then mix two-part epoxy with mica powder and add it to the fired metal clay. After the resin cures, you have a beautiful pair of earrings with that enamel look but without all the fuss. As pretty as these are, you may want a pair in every color.

MATERIALS

7½g low-fire metal clay

metal clay slip or paste

two-part epoxy (Loctite)

copper-colored mica powder (Jacquard Pearl Ex)

needle

2 sterling silver ear wires

basic metal clay tool kit (see page 17)

basic jewelry tool kit (see page 34)

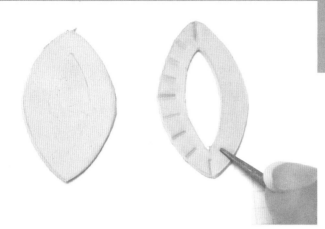

1. CUT CLAY

Prepare your hands and work surface for working with metal clay (see *Handling Clay*, page 18). Roll metal clay to a two-card thickness (see *Rolling Clay*, page 19). Cut 2 solid marquises from the metal clay using the outer line only of the marquise template for this project on page 126. Roll the remaining metal clay to a three-card thickness. Cut 2 open marquises from the metal clay using the inner and outer lines of the marquise template. Use the tip of a toothpick to indent the edges of each open marquise.

2. CONSTRUCT EARRING COMPONENTS

Allow all of the metal clay components to completely dry. Refine the inner edges of the open marquises (see *Refining Dry Clay*, page 29). Using slip, join an open marquise component to a closed marquise component (see *Layering Pieces of Clay*, page 24). Repeat for the second earring. Refine the outer edges of each piece, making sure the pieces are the same size and all of the joins are sealed. Use a small drill bit or craft knife to create a hole near the top point of each component (see *Creating Holes in Dry Clay*, page 28). Fire each piece individually, following the firing chart on page 14 (see *Firing Metal Clay with a Torch*, page 30). Burnish the metal with a soft brass brush (see *Brush Burnishing*, page 31).

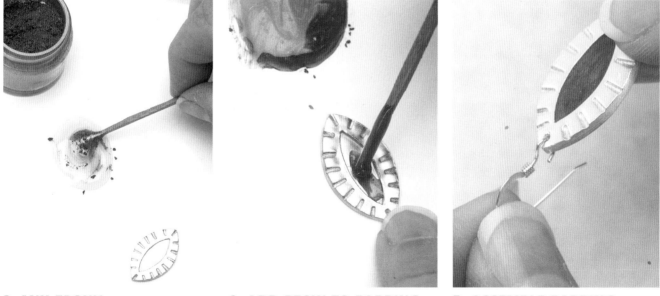

3. MIX EPOXY

Mix the epoxy according to the manufacturer's instructions. Thoroughly mix in mica powder until you reach the desired color.

4. ADD RESIN TO EARRING

Fill the well of each earring with the tinted epoxy (see *Adding Colored Two-Part Epoxy*, page 32). If there are bubbles in the epoxy, gently tap the earring on a hard surface so that the bubbles will rise to the surface of the epoxy. Pop any bubbles in the epoxy with a needle. Allow the epoxy to completely dry.

5. ASSEMBLE EARRING

Open the loop at the bottom of an ear wire, hook the finished component onto the loop and close the loop (see *Opening Ear Wires and Eye Pins*, page 36). Repeat for the second earring.

tip

Yard sales are a great place to find old jewelry or other items with interesting textures that can be used to make unique molds.

For this project, the mold is not of the fungus type but of the polymer clay type. I was inspired to create these earrings while on a vacation to Florida. I am always in awe of all the different colors and sizes of seashells on the beach. I am especially fond of the wee little ones that have made it through the vast ocean and onto the beach unscathed, just like the one I used to create my polymer clay mold. The neat thing about this project is that this special mold can be reused. The next time you are on vacation, take note of the textures around you. You may find something that is just screaming to become a piece of art.

MATERIALS

6g low-fire metal clay

seashell mold (see *Creating a Polymer Clay Mold*, page 19)

2 sterling silver ear wires

2 sterling silver head pins

2 mother-of-pearl chip beads

2 sterling silver spacer beads

basic metal clay tool kit (see page 17)

basic jewelry tool kit (see page 34)

1. MOLD CLAY

Lightly coat the inside of the seashell mold with olive oil or beeswax balm. Form half of the metal clay into a ball, then push it firmly into the seashell mold (see *Using a Mold*, page 19). Work your fingers across the clay, pushing it into every detail of the mold. Turn the mold clay side down onto the work surface. Hold down the excess clay with your finger and gently roll the mold off of the molded clay.

2. TRIM CLAY

Trim away the excess clay around the molded portion with a craft knife.

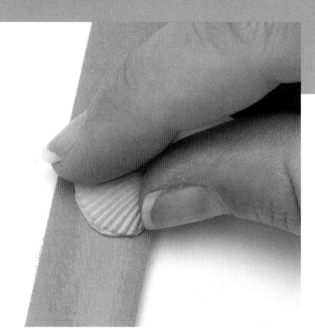

3. REFINE EDGES

Allow the molded clay to dry completely. Refine the back and edges of the dried piece (see *Refining Dry Clay*, page 29).

4. DRILL HOLE

Using a small drill bit, create a hole through the molded clay piece (see *Creating Holes in Dry Clay*, page 28). Drill at an angle to make the earring easier to assemble later.

5. FIRE CLAY

Repeat Steps 1 through 4 for a second seashell component. Fire each seashell individually following the firing chart on page 14 (see *Firing Metal Clay with a Torch*, page 30). Allow both pieces to cool completely. Burnish each seashell with a soft brass brush (see *Brush Burnishing*, page 31).

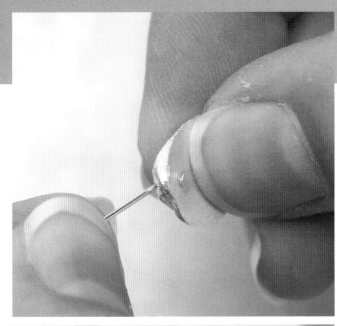

6. PLACE SEASHELL ON HEAD PIN

Slide a seashell component onto a head pin. Bend the end of the head pin back until the seashell hangs straight on the head pin. Place the seashell flat side down on the work surface and press on the seashell until the head on the head pin is flush with the back of the seashell.

7. ADD BEADS

Slide a chip bead and a spacer bead onto the head pin. Form the end of the head pin into a loop from the excess wire (see *Creating Loops in Head Pins and Eye Pins*, page 37).

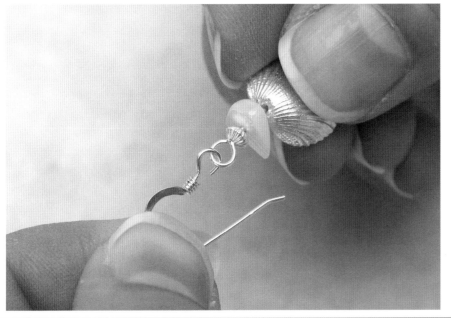

8. ASSEMBLE EARRINGS

Open the loop at the bottom of an ear wire, hook the head pin onto the loop, and close the loop (*Opening Ear Wires and Eye Pins*, page 36). Repeat Steps 6 through 8 for the second earring.

tip

Many different dried spices will work well in this project. Try paprika for a beautiful red-orange or turmeric for yellow.

Yes, you can believe it when I say you can make a bezel setting out of metal clay. Most bezels are made of silver bezel wire soldered to a base, but you can use the technique in this project to make a bezel out of a strip of metal clay. Join the clay strip into a ring and attach it to the base. Voila! You have a setting ready for a gemstone, or, in this case, a faux gemstone. Polymer clay, a very versatile medium, is wonderful for imitating all types of materials. This project shows you how to make a faux gemstone out of polymer clay using a common spice you have in your kitchen cabinet. Now that's a way to spice up metal clay!

MATERIALS

5½g low-fire metal clay

metal clay slip or paste

7/16" (11mm) diameter dowel rod or
    round spoon handle

lace doily

translucent polymer clay

ground pepper

1,000-grit wet/dry sandpaper

liver of sulfur

baking soda

2 glass containers

polishing cloth

2 sterling silver ear wires

basic metal clay tool kit (see page 17)

basic jewelry tool kit (see page 34)

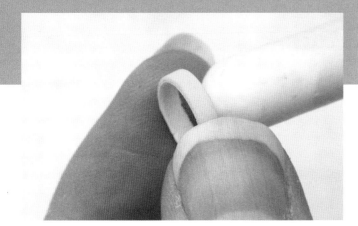

1. CREATE BEZEL

Prepare your hands and work surface for working with metal clay (see *Handling Clay*, page 18). Roll metal clay to a two-card thickness (see *Rolling Clay*, page 19). Using a straight blade, cut the clay to ⅛" × 1½" (3mm × 4cm). Apply a thin coat of olive oil or beeswax balm to the dowel rod or spoon handle and form the metal clay strip into a bezel around it, trimming the clay as needed (see *Creating Bezels*, page 25). Allow the bezel to dry completely.

2. CREATE BASE

Roll the remaining metal clay to a four-card thickness. Place the lace doily on top of the rolled clay; roll over the clay and doily with a roller to impress the doily pattern into the clay. Remove the doily from the clay, and use the round template for this project on page 126 to cut the clay base. Align the template with the center of the doily pattern. Brush a line of water on the bottom rim of the bezel and on the base where the bezel will be located. Join the bezel to the base. Allow the clay to completely dry. Refine the edges of the base and bezel, and drill a hole in the base with a small drill bit or craft knife (see *Refining Dry Clay*, page 29 and *Creating Holes in Dry Clay*, page 28). Repeat Steps 1 and 2 for the second earring. Compare the pieces to ensure they are the same size. If the pieces do not match, file the larger piece to match the smaller.

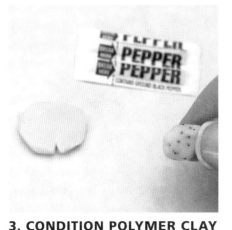

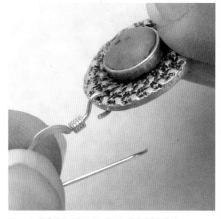

3. CONDITION POLYMER CLAY

Fire each metal clay piece individually following the firing chart on page 14 (see *Firing Metal Clay with a Torch*, page 30). Burnish both with a soft brass brush (see *Brush Burnishing*, page 31). To prepare the polymer clay to fill the bezel, condition the translucent polymer clay and mix it with ground pepper, replicating the appearance of a semiprecious stone.

4. FILL BEZEL

Roll the prepared polymer clay into 2 pea-sized balls. Push 1 piece of polymer clay into each bezel so that the clay is mounded in the bezel. Roll the clay on the work surface to shape it into a cabochon. Bake the earrings at 250° F (120° C) for 30 minutes. Allow the earring dangles to cool completely. Lightly sand the polymer clay with wet 1,000-grit wet/dry sandpaper, then buff vigourously on denim until the polymer clay shines like a polished stone.

5. ASSEMBLE EARRINGS

Patinate each earring with liver of sulfur (see *Using Liver of Sulfur*, page 33). Open the loop at the bottom of an ear wire, hook a metal clay piece onto the loop and close the loop (see *Opening Ear Wires and Eye Pins*, page 36). Repeat for the second earring.

galactic cylinder earrings

When I created this project, it did not occur to me what these beads "wanted" to be until I finished the silver and assembled them with beads. Adding a textured ring around the center of these basic barrel-shaped earrings gives them a kind of spacecraft look, so of course they had to be named accordingly. These earrings look as if they are ready to take flight, right off of an earlobe. Try your hand at these earrings, and have a close encounter of the metal clay kind.

MATERIALS

7g low-fire metal clay

metal clay slip and paste

drinking straw or 7mm diameter dowel rod

nylon scrub pad

2" (5cm) length of ball chain

polymer clay

2 sterling silver ear wires

2 sterling silver head pins

4 size 11/0 green seed beads

basic metal clay tool kit (see page 17)

basic jewelry tool kit (see page 34)

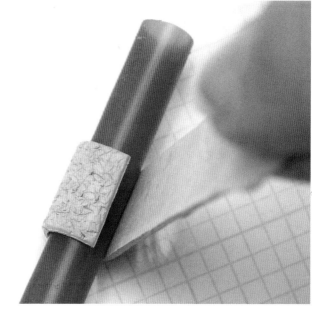

1. TEXTURE CLAY

Prepare your hands and work surface for working with metal clay (see *Handling Clay*, page 18). Roll metal clay to a four-card thickness (see *Rolling Clay*, page 19). Dab the rolled metal clay with a nylon scrub pad for texture.

2. TRIM CLAY

Using a straight blade, cut the clay to ½" × 1½" (1cm × 4cm). Apply a thin coat of olive oil or beeswax balm to the straw or dowel rod, and roll the metal clay strip into a cylinder around the straw or dowel rod. Trim the clay so that the ends meet without overlapping.

3. FORM CYLINDER

Join the ends of the metal clay strip with paste to form a cylinder around the straw or dowel (see *Joining Clay to Form Cylinders*, page 25). Sand and reseal the join as needed. Allow the clay cylinder to dry completely, and remove it from the dowel or straw.

4. JOIN CLAY TO CYLINDER ENDS

Roll metal clay to a four-card thickness. Dab the rolled metal clay with a nylon scrubbing pad for texture. Turn the clay over on your work surface. Brush a line of slip around one end of the clay cylinder. Lightly press the dried clay cylinder into the fresh clay. Using the clay cylinder as a template, cut the rolled clay.

5. SEAL JOINS

Brush a thin layer of paste around the join between the clay cylinder and the clay disk. Allow the paste to dry for several seconds, then dab the join with a nylon scrubbing pad to match the texture of the join to that of the rest of the cylinder. Repeat Steps 4 and 5 on the other end of the cylinder. Allow the cylinder to dry completely.

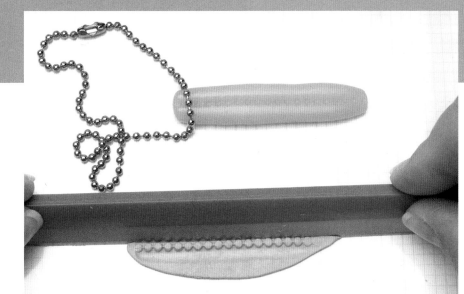

6. MOLD CLAY

Create a 1½" (4cm) mold of a piece of ball chain using polymer clay (see *Creating and Using Molds*, pages 19-20). Coat the mold with a thin layer of olive oil or beeswax balm. Roll the remaining metal clay into a snake and press it firmly into the mold. Cut the excess clay away from either side of the molded clay.

7. ADD MOLDED CLAY

Brush a line of water around the center of the dried clay cylinder and on the back of the molded clay. Join the molded clay to the clay cylinder in a ring around the center of the cylinder. Allow the clay to dry completely. Seal any cracks or gaps in the joins. Using a craft knife, drill a hole in the center of each end of the cylinder (see *Creating Holes in Dry Clay*, page 28).

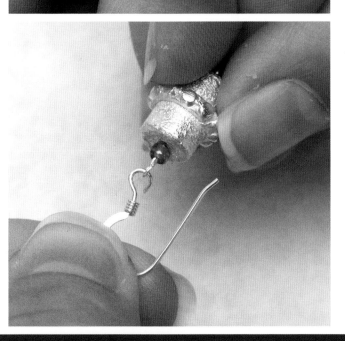

8. COMPLETE EARRINGS

Repeat Steps 1 through 7 to make a second cylinder. Fire each cylinder individually following the firing chart on page 14 (see *Firing Metal Clay with a Torch*, page 30). Allow both pieces to cool completely. Burnish each cylinder with a soft brass brush (see *Brush Burnishing*, page 31). To assemble an earring, slide a seed bead, a metal cylinder and a second seed bead onto a head pin. Close the end of the head pin with a loop (see *Creating Loops in Head Pins and Eye Pins*, page 37). Open the loop at the bottom of an ear wire, hook the head pin onto the loop, and close the loop (see *Opening Ear Wires and Eye Pins*, page 36). Repeat for the second earring.

starry cone earrings

These lovely earrings have so much design potential! I used a simple Phillips screwdriver to make starlike impressions in the metal clay, but you can use the metal clay as a canvas to create any design you like. Search your house for other everyday objects to give your metal clay creation a unique look. A variety of beads will look great with this design, as well. The simple black onyx I chose creates a classic, elegant look, but these earrings can be easily modified to fit your own taste and wardrobe. There are as many options for these fun earrings as there are stars in the sky.

MATERIALS

7g low-fire metal clay
metal clay slip or paste
lightweight cardstock
Phillips head screwdriver
2 sterling silver ear wires
2 sterling silver head pins
2 6mm spacer beads
2 8mm × 10mm black onyx beads
basic metal clay tool kit (see page 17)
basic jewelry tool kit (see page 34)

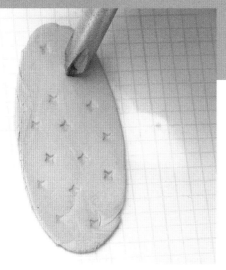

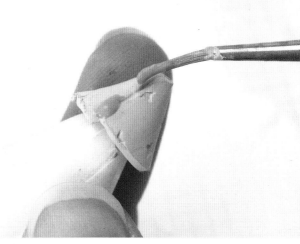

1. PREPARE CLAY

Using the support template for this project on page 126, create from lightweight cardstock a cone to support the metal clay. Prepare your hands and work surface for working with metal clay (see *Handling Clay*, page 18). Roll metal clay to a four-card thickness (see *Rolling Clay*, page 19). Make several impressions in the rolled clay with the tip of a Phillips screwdriver.

2. FORM CONE

Cut the metal clay using the cone template for this project on page 126. Apply a thin coat of olive oil or beeswax balm to the cardstock cone. Join the edges of the metal clay with paste to form a cone around the cardstock support (see *Joining Clay to Form Cylinders*, page 25). Sand and reseal the join as needed. Allow the clay cone to dry completely.

3. REFINE EDGES

Sand the top and bottom edges of the cone until they are smooth and level (see *Refining Dry Clay*, page 29). Use the tip of a craft knife to refine the hole in the top of the cone. Repeat Steps 1 through 3 to make a second cone. Place the cones side by side and make sure they match in size. If they do not, sand the larger to match the smaller.

4. ASSEMBLE EARRINGS

Fire each cone individually following the firing chart on page 14 (see *Firing Metal Clay with a Torch*, page 30). Allow both pieces to cool completely. Burnish each cone with a soft brass brush (see *Brush Burnishing*, page 31). Slide a black onyx bead, a spacer bead and a metal cone onto a head pin. Make a loop at the end of the head pin (see *Creating Loops in Head Pins and Eye Pins*, page 37). Open the loop at the bottom of an ear wire, hook the head pin onto the loop, and close the loop (see *Opening Ear Wires and Eye Pins*, page 36). Repeat for the second earring.

NOTABLE
NECKWEAR

Necklaces, neckwear or neckpieces, whatever you want to call them, have been around since ancient times. Archeologists believe the necklace was born during the Stone Age. When scientists were excavating a cave in South Africa, they discovered mollusks that may have been strung as neck jewelry about 75,000 years ago. Before this discovery the oldest known necklace was believed to have been made approximately 32,000 years ago. Early necklaces were made mostly of shells, bones, stones, animal teeth or claws strung on a thread. In Egypt archeologists have also found silver objects dating back nearly 5,500 years. Drawings on some of the oldest pyramids show men working with metal, probably extracting silver from its ores to make beautiful jewelry for their kings and queens. Other early cultures also used silver. Written records from India describe the metal as far back as 3,000 years ago. Silver was also common in the Americas when Europeans first arrived.

Today, with the acceptance of mixed media as an art form, you can find necklaces made of just about any kind of material. Because silver is an attractive metal, it is widely used for beads and other objects to be incorporated into fantastic works of art, especially in the jewelry industry. In this chapter, you can learn how to make several different pendants and necklaces to wear as-is or to incorporate with other media. From the stunning simplicity of the *Rip It, Rip It Good Pendant* (page 68) to the intricate beauty of the *Tantalizing Teardrop Necklace* (page 92), this chapter has a wide range of projects suitable for every skill level. These projects are easy to learn, and I encourage you to add a bit of your own creative pizzazz to them. That, after all, is what will make your jewelry creation an original, one-of-a-kind piece for you to show, admire and wear for years to come.

rip it, rip it good pendant

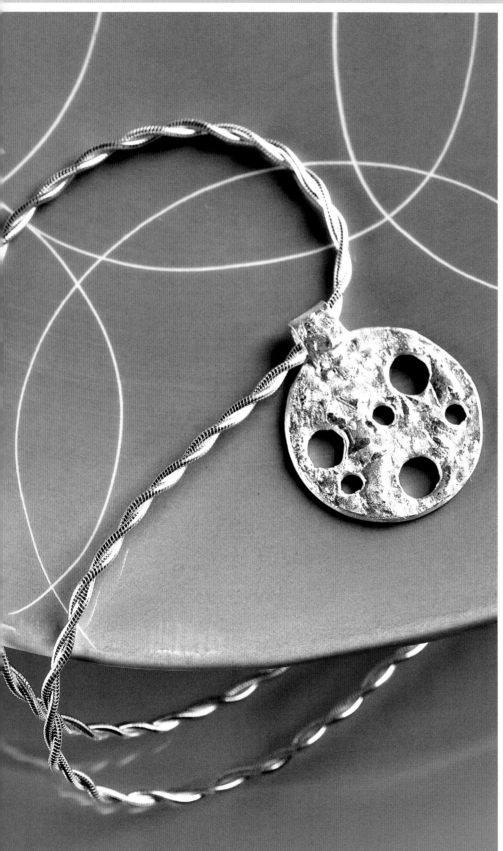

Those of you who grew up in the 1980s may remember how a popular tune called "Whip It" would play over and over again in your head after you heard it on the radio. Coincidentally, that song was the inspiration for the name of this pendant because you will want to use the techniques from this project over and over again. This is a nice, quick project that is almost effortless. The main tools for this project? Your hands. By tearing thin sheets of metal clay and layering them, you create an interesting organic look. I say rip it, rip it good!

MATERIALS

PENDANT

5½g low-fire metal clay

metal clay slip or paste

thin stir straw and drinking straw

metal spoon

basic metal clay tool kit (see page 17)

NECKLACE VARIATION

same as pendant, plus:

oil paint

paper towel

22" (56cm) length of beading wire

2 sterling silver crimp tubes

1 sterling silver jump ring

1 sterling silver lobster claw clasp

approximately 175 size 6/0 red and pink seed beads

basic jewelry tool kit (see page 34)

  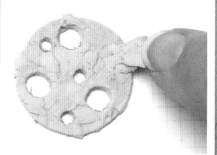

1. LAYER CLAY

Prepare your hands and work surface for working with metal clay (see *Handling Clay*, page 18). Roll metal clay to a three-card thickness (see *Rolling Clay*, page 19). Cut the metal clay using the template for this project on page 126. Roll the remaining metal clay to a one-card thickness. Brush the entire surface of the clay circle with a thin coat of slip. Tear small pieces of clay from the thinly rolled clay, then layer them on the clay circle.

2. CREATE HOLES

Brush a thin coat of water over the surface of the pendant, sealing the torn clay pieces to the clay circle. Begin punching holes in the pendant using the stir straw and the drinking straw, leaving a solid space of clay for attaching the bail (see *Creating Holes in Wet Clay*, page 28). Dry the clay completely and refine the inner and outer edges of the pendant (see *Refining Dry Clay*, page 29).

3. ATTACH BAIL

Roll the remaining metal clay to a two-card thickness. Cut a ¼" × ¾" (6mm × 2cm) strip of clay. Join the clay strip to the front and back of the clay circle, forming a sandwich bail (see *Creating a Sandwich Bail*, page 27). Disguise the area where the bail joins the pendant with torn pieces of clay, as in Step 1. Allow the clay to dry completely. Refine the edges of the bail.

4. BURNISH PENDANT

Fire the pendant following the firing chart on page 14 (see *Firing Metal Clay with a Torch*, page 30). Allow the metal to cool completely. Burnish the pendant, first with a soft brass brush, then with the back of a metal spoon (see *Burnishing*, page 31).

necklace variation

For this necklace, I applied black oil paint to the pendant for a faux patina (see Adding Oil Paint, *page 32) and made it a part of a beaded necklace. To make this necklace, attach the beading wire to the clasp with a crimp tube (see* Crimping, *page 37). String 8½" (22cm) of seed beads, then slide the pendant onto the beading wire. String another 8½" (22cm) of seed beads onto the beading wire, then crimp a jump ring onto the end of the beading wire.*

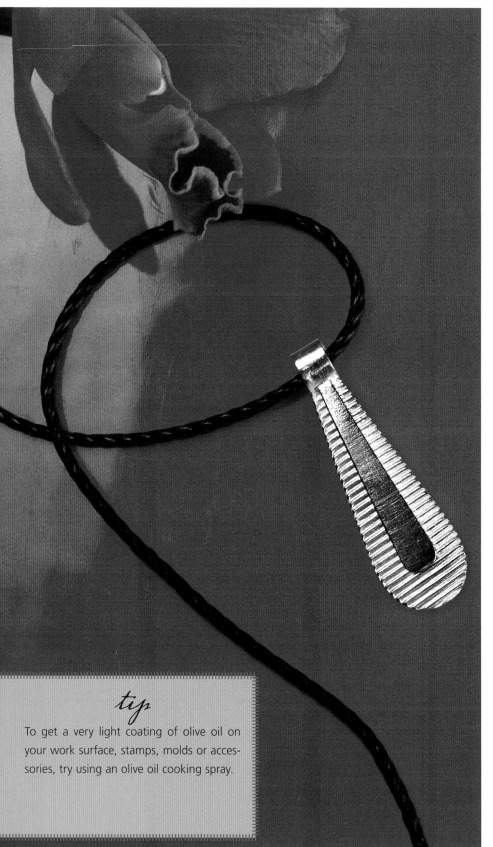

The idea for this pendant came to me one morning while I was brushing my teeth. I was starting a new project and wanted to include an interesting texture. I looked at the cap on my tube of toothpaste and wondered what kind of texture it would create on metal clay. Because I was so excited when I saw how well the texture worked, I decided to make this pendant in the shape of an exclamation point (upside down). Thus, this metal clay piece was born. This pendant has a nice clean shape and looks great alone as a pendant or strung as part of a necklace. So when you finish that tube of toothpaste, do not flip your lid in the trash; use it to make interesting jewelry.

MATERIALS

5g low-fire metal clay

metal clay slip and paste

5mm diameter dowel rod or drinking straw

ridged bottle cap

basic metal clay tool kit (see page 17)

tip

To get a very light coating of olive oil on your work surface, stamps, molds or accessories, try using an olive oil cooking spray.

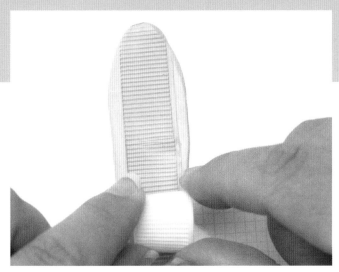

1. TEXTURE CLAY

Prepare your hands and work surface for working with metal clay (see *Handling Clay*, page 18). Roll metal clay to a two-card thickness (see *Rolling Clay*, page 19). Cut the metal clay using the smaller template for this project on page 126. Allow the metal clay to dry completely. Refine the edges of this clay piece (see *Refining Dry Clay*, page 29). Roll the remaining metal clay to a four-card thickness. Roll a ridged bottle cap on its side over the clay. Cut the metal clay using the larger template for this project on page 126.

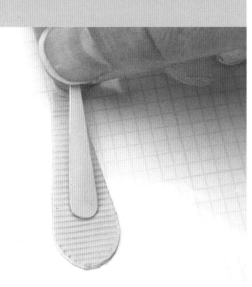

2. JOIN LAYERS

Brush slip over the center of the ridged clay piece and onto the back of the dried clay piece. Join the small, dried clay piece to the large, ridged clay piece (see *Layering Pieces of Clay*, page 24). Seal all of the edges where the clay joins together. Allow the clay to dry completely. Refine the edges of the larger clay piece.

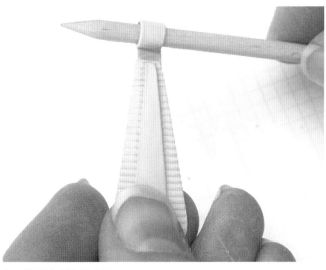

3. ATTACH BAIL

Roll the remaining metal clay to a three-card thickness and cut a ⁷/₃₂" × ¾" (6mm × 2cm) strip from the clay. Form the clay strip into a tube bail with a tail around the dowel rod or straw (see *Creating a Tube Bail with a Tail*, page 27). Allow the bail to dry completely. Refine the edges of the bail. Join the bail to the pendant with metal clay paste. Allow the clay to completely dry.

4. FIRE PENDANT

Fire the pendant following the firing chart on page 14 (see *Firing Metal Clay with a Torch*, page 30). Allow the metal to cool completely. Burnish the pendant with a soft brass brush (see *Brush Burnishing*, page 31).

initial it necklace

Most people love personalized jewelry, and here you have the chance to create such an item. My daughter adores having jewelry and other items with her name or initial on them; she has an uncommon name, so you can imagine how many things I have had to make instead of buy over the years. I came by the texture for this piece in an odd sort of way: While getting apples from my refrigerator, I happened to notice the nonslip rubber shelf liner the apples were resting on. I thought it could be used to create a neat checkerboard design, so I decided to experiment with it. With the mat, a rubber alphabet stamp and a little bit of epoxy in hand, I created this beautiful initial pendant. These are great for gifts—I know mine suits me to a T!

MATERIALS

6g low-fire metal clay
metal clay slip or paste
nonslip shelf liner
alphabet rubber stamp
two-part epoxy (Loctite)
metallic purple acrylic paint
   (Jacquard Lumiere)
2 sterling silver jump rings
18" (46cm) silver chain with clasp
basic metal clay tool kit (see page 17)
basic jewelry tool kit (see page 34)

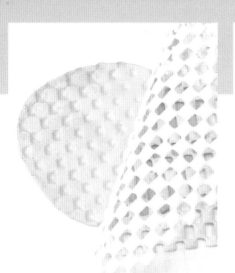

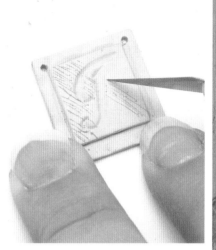

1. TEXTURE CLAY

Prepare your hands and work surface for working with metal clay (see *Handling Clay*, page 18). Roll metal clay to a four-card thickness (see *Rolling Clay*, page 19). Apply a light coat of olive oil or beeswax balm to the nonslip shelf liner and press it into the rolled metal clay. Roll over the shelf liner and clay with the roller to create an even impression. Gently peel the liner off of the clay. Cut a ⁷⁄₈" × ⁷⁄₈" (2cm × 2cm) square from the textured clay.

2. JOIN CLAY PIECES

Roll the remaining metal clay to a three-card thickness. Apply a light coat of olive oil or beeswax balm to the alphabet stamp and press it into the rolled metal clay. Cut a ⁵⁄₈" × ⁵⁄₈" (16mm × 16mm) square around the stamped letter. Allow the stamped square of clay to dry completely. Refine the edges of the stamped clay (see *Refining Dry Clay*, page 29). Join the stamped piece of clay to the textured piece of clay (see *Layering Pieces of Clay*, page 24).

3. SCRATCH DRIED CLAY

Allow the clay to dry completely. Refine the edges of the larger square. Use a small drill or craft knife to create two holes in the top of the pendant (see *Creating Holes in Dry Clay*, page 28). Scratch the stamped clay square diagonally with the tip of a craft knife.

4. ADD EPOXY TO PENDANT

Fire the pendant following the firing chart on page 14 (see *Firing Metal Clay with a Torch*, page 30). Allow the metal to cool completely. Burnish the pendant with a soft brass brush (see *Brush Burnishing*, page 31). Mix the two-part epoxy according to the manufacturer's instructions. Mix metallic purple paint into the two-part epoxy until you reach the color you desire (see *Adding Colored Two-Part Epoxy*, page 32). Using a toothpick, drip the tinted epoxy into the stamped letter. Allow the two-part epoxy to dry completely.

5. ASSEMBLE NECKLACE

Open a jump ring and hook it through a hole in the pendant and through a link in the silver chain (see *Opening and Closing Jump Rings*, page 36). Close the jump ring. Repeat on the other side of the pendant.

hip to be square necklace

Here is a necklace that will leave you feeling hip to be square. Yes, I know that sounds a bit corny. However, with my love of music, I often have random tunes running through my head. Taking a look at this finished piece of geometric shapes, I could not resist that title. This project gets its texture from an interesting handmade tool: a carved piece of eraser. Erasers come in handy for creating customized stamps, so I used a craft knife to carve a small square on the end of a piece of eraser. To add a bit of pizzazz, I added some colorful beads to this necklace. Try this necklace; you don't have to be a square to wear squares.

MATERIALS

6g low-fire metal clay

metal clay slip or paste

eraser

metal spoon

22" (56cm) length of beading wire

2 sterling silver crimp tubes

5 sterling silver jump rings

1 sterling silver lobster claw clasp

approximately 200 size 8/0 green, blue, pink and red seed beads

basic metal clay tool kit (see page 17)

basic jewelry tool kit (see page 34)

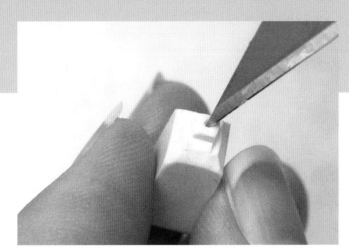

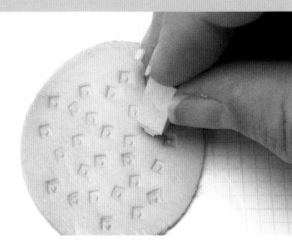

1. CARVE STAMP

Using a craft knife, carve an eraser to make a stamp of your choice. Here, I carved a ⅛"× ⅛"(3mm × 3mm) square with a 1mm-diameter hole in the center.

2. STAMP CLAY

Prepare your hands and work surface for working with metal clay (see *Handling Clay*, page 18). Roll metal clay to a four-card thickness (see *Rolling Clay*, page 19). Apply a thin layer of olive oil or beeswax balm to the eraser stamp. Stamp the rolled metal clay repeatedly. Cut a ¾" × ¾" (2cm × 2cm) square from the textured clay. Cut a ⅜"× ⅜" (1cm × 1cm) square out of the center of the clay square. Make sure to handle the clay carefully, as you will use both squares in the necklace.

3. CUT CLAY PIECES

Roll the remaining metal clay to a three-card thickness. Stamp the rolled metal clay repeatedly with the eraser stamp. Cut a ⁵⁄₁₆"× ⁵⁄₁₆" (8mm × 8mm) square from the textured clay. Allow this square to dry, then refine its outer edges (see *Refining Dry Clay*, page 29). Roll the remaining metal clay to a three-card thickness and cut a ½" (13mm) square from the untextured clay. Join the ⁵⁄₁₆"× ⁵⁄₁₆" (8mm × 8mm) textured square to the ½" × ½" (13mm × 13mm) untextured square (see *Layering Pieces of Clay*, page 24). Allow all of the clay pieces to dry completely. Refine the edges of each piece. Using a small drill bit or craft knife, drill holes in the following locations: 2 holes in the top and 1 hole in the bottom of the open square; 1 hole at the top and bottom of the layered square; 1 hole at the top of the smallest square (see *Creating Holes in Dry Clay*, page 28).

4. ASSEMBLE NECKLACE

Fire the clay pieces individually following the firing chart on page 14 (see *Firing Metal Clay with a Torch*, page 30). Allow the metal to cool completely. Burnish the pieces first with a soft brass brush, then with the back of a metal spoon (see *Burnishing*, page 31). Attach the beading wire to the clasp with a crimp tube (see *Crimping*, page 37). String the seed beads to form an 18" (46cm) necklace. Crimp a jump ring onto the end of the beading wire. Join the 3 pieces of metal clay together with jump rings (see *Opening and Closing Jump Rings*, page 36). Join the metal pieces to the beaded necklace with jump rings.

oh, swirly-q pendant

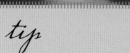

tip

Never throw away metal clay flakes or powder from your work area or wrappers. Collect them and put them in your slip jar with a little bit of distilled water and a drop of vinegar to always have slip on hand.

I am a big fan of circle, swirl and curl designs, which is why I am so drawn to this piece of jewelry. There is just something about these design elements that makes me happy, and I guess that it may have something to do with my psychedelic character. This project uses a childhood pastime, rolling clay snakes, to create a beautiful necklace for your grown-up self. Who knew you could have so much fun playing with clay outside of grade school art?

MATERIALS

PENDANT

8½g low-fire metal clay

metal clay slip and paste

basic metal clay tool kit (see page 17)

NECKLACE VARIATION

8½g low-fire metal clay

metal clay slip and paste

22" (56cm) length of beading wire

2 sterling silver crimp tubes

1 sterling silver jump ring

1 sterling silver lobster claw clasp

approximately 175 size 6/0 orange, yellow and clear seed beads

basic metal clay tool kit (see page 17)

basic jewelry tool kit (see page 34)

1. ROLL SNAKE

Prepare your hands and work surface for working with metal clay (see *Handling Clay*, page 18). Set aside a pea-size ball of metal clay for the bail. Roll the remaining clay into a long tapered snake that is 5" (13cm). Begin rolling the snake by hand, but finish by rolling with a flat surface, such as the lid of a tin or a deck of cards.

2. COIL SNAKE

Brush a line of water along a side of the metal clay snake. Beginning with the thick end, wind the clay snake into a tight coil. Gently press the layers together as you roll the coil.

77

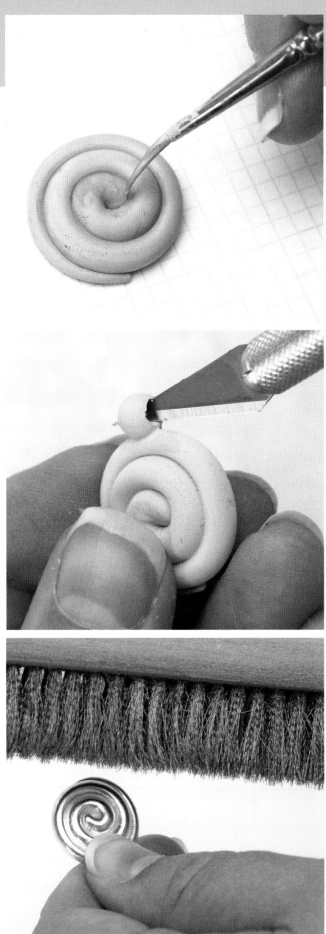

3. SEAL SNAKE

Brush slip along the coil where the rounds of clay meet to seal the layers of clay together. Use the paintbrush to smooth out any imperfections in the clay.

4. ATTACH BAIL

Roll the reserved clay into a ball. Use paste to join the ball of clay to the clay coil to form a ball bail (see *Creating a Ball Bail*, page 27). Allow the clay to dry completely. Use a craft knife to drill a hole through the bail (see *Creating Holes in Dry Clay*, page 28). Refine and smooth any rough edges (see *Refining Dry Clay*, page 29).

5. COMPLETE PENDANT

Fire the pendant following the firing chart on page 14 (see *Firing Metal Clay with a Torch*, page 30). Allow the metal to cool completely. Burnish the pendant with a soft brass brush (see *Brush Burnishing*, page 31).

necklace variation

I always enjoy color in a project, so for an unadorned silver pendant like this one I like to string a beaded necklace. To make this necklace, attach the beading wire to the clasp with a crimp tube (see Crimping, page 37). String 8½" (22cm) of seed beads, then slide the pendant onto the beading wire. String another 8½" (22cm) of seed beads onto the necklace, then crimp a jump ring onto the end of the beading wire. To customize the length of this necklace change the beading wire length and use more or fewer beads on either side of the pendant.

This stunning necklace was named after the item I used for the texture: string. To be more exact, I used ordinary twine to make impressions in metal clay. I found that by pressing the string into the metal clay I could get a nice ropelike imprint, a sort of nautical look. When I used a mother-of-pearl disk bead as a template for making my metal clay disks, I noticed that the mother-of-pearl would add a nice touch to the nautical theme because of its aquatic origins. Although I am partial to the mother-of-pearl, disk beads made from other materials would look just as fabulous in this design. "Sea" to it that you make a necklace that suits you.

MATERIALS

20g low-fire metal clay

thick cotton twine

18 6mm oval sterling silver jump rings

1 sterling silver S clasp

3" (8cm) segment sterling silver chain

10 1½" (4cm) mother-of-pearl disk beads

basic metal clay tool kit (see page 17)

basic jewelry tool kit (see page 34)

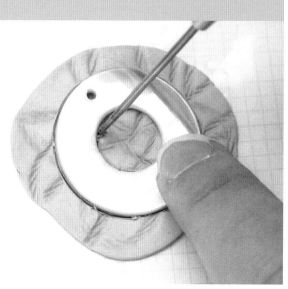

1. TEXTURE CLAY

Prepare your hands and work surface for working with metal clay (see *Handling Clay*, page 18). Roll metal clay to a four-card thickness (see *Rolling Clay*, page 19). Apply a thin layer of olive oil or balm to the twine. Randomly arrange the twine on the rolled clay. Press the twine into the clay with the roller. Make sure you don't press too hard and thin the clay.

2. CUT CLAY

Using a mother-of-pearl disk bead as a template, cut the metal clay (see *Cutting Curved Lines*, page 22).

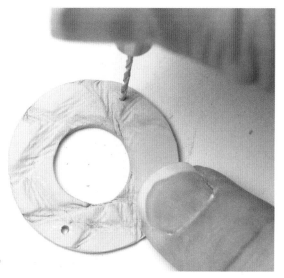

3. REFINE DISK

Allow the clay to dry completely. Refine the inner and outer edges of the clay (see *Refining Dry Clay*, page 29). Using a small drill bit, drill 2 holes opposite each other in the disk (see *Creating Holes in Dry Clay*, page 28). Repeat Steps 1 through 3 to create a total of 5 clay disks.

Fire the clay pieces individually following the firing chart on page 14 (see *Firing Metal Clay with a Torch*, page 30). Allow the metal to cool completely. Burnish the disks with a soft brass brush (see *Brush Burnishing*, page 31).

4. ASSEMBLE NECKLACE

To assemble the necklace, connect the mother-of-pearl disks and the metal disks with jump rings in the following order: 3 mother-of-pearl disks, 1 metal disk, then alternate 1 mother-of-pearl disk and 1 metal disk 4 times, then end with 3 mother-of-pearl disks (see *Opening and Closing Jump Rings*, page 36). Connect a 1" (3cm) segment of chain to each end of the necklace with a jump ring. Connect a jump ring to the end of each segment of chain. Slide an S clasp onto one of the jump rings and pinch that side of the clasp closed. Leave the other side of the clasp open for connecting the ends of the necklace.

This is a beautiful and fun project with a very organic look that really brings me back to nature. Believing in nature and all of its bounties is very important to me. Mother Nature has provided us with food, medicine and a picturesque earth with a fabulous color palette. You can further share in the beauty of nature by molding a twig in fine silver and by using the veins of a small leaf to texture your metal clay. You can choose from a wide array of leaf forms to suit your taste. Once you assemble your pieces you can not only look at nature but wear it, too.

MATERIALS

5½g low-fire metal clay

leaf

small twig

polymer clay

liver of sulfur

baking soda

2 glass containers

polishing cloth

8" (20cm) length of 22-gauge copper wire (Artishtic Wire Ltd)

basic metal clay tool kit (see page 17)

basic jewelry tool kit (see page 34)

tip

Keep a chunk of polymer clay or two-part silicone molding compound on hand when you travel. You never know when you may stumble on an object you would like to mold.

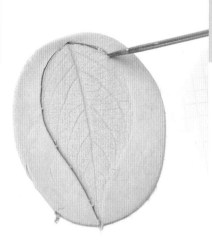

1. STAMP CLAY

Prepare your hands and work surface for working with metal clay (see *Handling Clay*, page 18). Roll metal clay to a four-card thickness (see *Rolling Clay*, page 19). Apply a thin layer of olive oil or beeswax balm to a leaf. Press the bottom side of the leaf into the rolled metal clay with a roller. Gently peel the leaf off of the clay.

2. CUT LEAF

Using a needle tool, cut freehand around the outline of the leaf in the metal clay. Allow the clay to completely dry. Refine the edges of the clay leaf (see *Refining Dry Clay*, page 29). Using a small drill bit or craft knife, drill a hole near the top of the leaf (see *Creating Holes in Dry Clay*, page 28).

3. MOLD CLAY

Create a polymer clay mold of a small twig (see *Creating and Using Molds*, pages 19-20). Coat the mold with a thin layer of olive oil or beeswax balm. Roll the remaining metal clay into a snake and press it firmly into the mold. Remove the clay from the mold and cut the excess clay away from either side of the molded clay. Allow the molded clay to dry completely. Refine the back and edges of the molded clay.

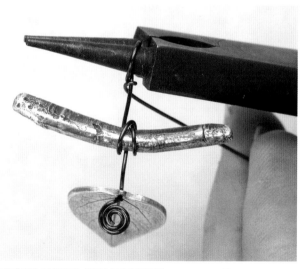

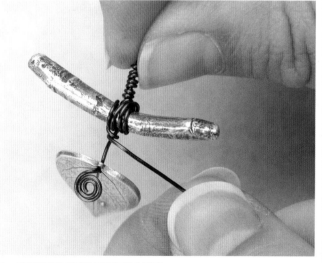

4. BEGIN WIRE WRAPPING

Fire the clay pieces individually following the firing chart on page 14 (see *Firing Metal Clay with a Torch*, page 30). Allow the metal to cool completely. Burnish the leaf and twig with a soft brass brush (see *Brush Burnishing*, page 31). Patinate both fired pieces with liver of sulfur (see *Using Liver of Sulfur*, page 33). Create a coil at 1 end of the copper wire. Slide the metal leaf onto the wire. Wrap the copper wire twice around the metal twig ¼" (6mm) above the leaf. Make a loop in the wire ¼" (6mm) above the twig. Begin coiling the remaining wire tail around the wire below the loop.

5. COMPLETE PENDANT

Continue to coil the wire tail downward around the wire until you reach the twig. Wrap the wire tail twice more around the twig, then continue coiling the wire tail around the wire downward toward the leaf. Once you have coiled the wire tail all the way down to the leaf, trim off the excess wire tail.

totally tubular necklace

I guess I am showing my age by using 1980s slang. The expression "totally tubular" was lost in the 1980s, seemingly never to return … until now. This necklace gives that phrase a whole new meaning. This project uses a few unexpected items to create fine silver tubes that will have much more staying power than 1980s slang. These tube beads look great in a variety of sizes, and they can be used on their own or with other items to create beautiful jewelry. They also look *totally awesome* with a patina, making this project *really radical*, if you know what I mean.

MATERIALS

16g low-fire metal clay

metal clay slip and paste

nylon scrub pad

⁷⁄₁₆" (11mm) diameter dowel rod or spoon handle

metal spoon

basic metal clay tool kit (see page 17)

1. TEXTURE CLAY

Prepare your hands and work surface for working with metal clay (see *Handling Clay*, page 18). Roll metal clay to a four-card thickness (see *Rolling Clay*, page 19). Dab the rolled metal clay with a nylon scrub pad for texture.

2. FORM TUBE

Using a straight blade, cut the clay to 1" × 1½" (3cm × 4cm). Apply a thin coat of olive oil or beeswax balm to the dowel rod or spoon handle and roll the metal clay strip into a cylinder around it. Trim the clay so that the ends meet without overlapping. Join the ends of the metal clay strip with paste to form a cylinder around the dowel rod or spoon handle (see *Joining Clay to Form Cylinders*, page 25). Using a needle tool, cut decorative holes in the cylinder.

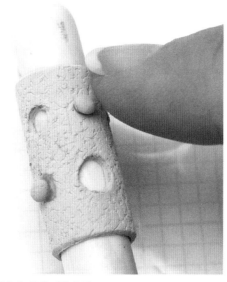

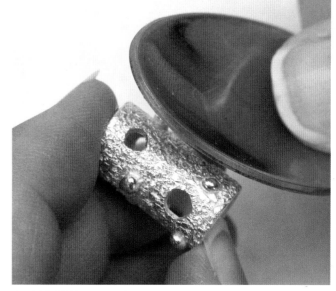

3. ATTACH BALLS OF CLAY

Roll several small balls from the remaining metal clay. Join the clay balls to the cylinder with metal clay paste. Seal the edges where the pieces of clay meet. Allow the clay to dry completely. Refine the edges of the cylinder and the inside edges of the decorative holes (see *Refining Dry Clay*, page 29). Repeat Steps 1 through 3 twice more with ¾" × 1½" (2cm × 4cm) strips of clay to create 2 small cylinders; omit the decorative holes.

4. FINISH TUBES

Fire the clay pieces individually following the firing chart on page 14 (see *Firing Metal Clay with a Torch*, page 30). Allow the metal to cool completely. Burnish the pieces first with a soft brass brush, then with the back of a metal spoon (see *Burnishing*, page 31). String the tubes on a chain or beaded strand to complete the necklace.

resin—ating dots pendant

Dots are a very popular design element in clothing and fashion accessories. You can find dots on items from fabric to furniture and everything in between. Dots, or polka dots, became very common in the late nineteenth century when polka music was popular, and they seem to have stood the test of time. This fun and interesting project using dots will also stand the test of time. Adding two-part epoxy mixed with metallic paints makes this project even more beautiful and fashionable. Try different color combinations in the resin to make this pendant your own.

MATERIALS

6g low-fire metal clay
metal clay slip or paste
thin stir straw
drinking straw
metal spoon
two-part epoxy (Loctite)
blue metallic ink (Posh Inkabilities)
purple metallic ink (Posh Inkabilities)
basic metal clay tool kit (see page 17)

tip

You can easily make your own needle tool from polymer clay and a large sewing needle. Use chain-nose pliers to bend the blunt end of the needle 45 degrees, then form polymer clay around the bent end of the needle to create a handle. Bake the piece following the polymer clay manufacturer's instructions, and you will have your own custom-made needle tool.

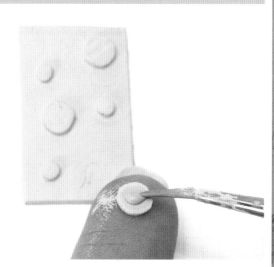

1. CUT CLAY COMPONENTS

Prepare your hands and work surface for working with metal clay (see *Handling Clay*, page 18). Roll metal clay to a four-card thickness (see *Rolling Clay*, page 19). Cut a ¾" × 1¼" (2cm × 3cm) rectangle from the clay. Roll the remaining metal clay to a three-card thickness. Make 3 impressions each in this rolled clay with the drinking straw and the stir straw. Cut with a needle tool along the impressions in the clay and remove the 6 circles.

2. JOIN CLAY PIECES

Allow the rectangle and the circles of clay to dry completely. Refine the edges of the clay circles (see *Refining Dry Clay*, page 29). Join the clay circles to the rectangle with metal clay paste (see *Layering Pieces of Clay*, page 24). Seal all of the edges where the clay pieces join. Allow the clay to completely dry. Refine the edges of the rectangle.

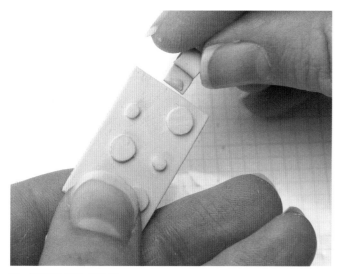

3. ATTACH BAIL

Roll the remaining metal clay to a three-card thickness and cut a ¾" × ¼" (2cm × 6mm) strip from the clay. Form the clay strip into a tube bail with a tail around the stir straw (see *Tube Bail with a Tail*, page 27). Allow the bail to dry completely. Refine the edges of the bail. Join the tail of the bail to the decorated clay rectangle with metal clay paste. Allow the clay to completely dry.

4. COMPLETE PENDANT

Fire the pendant following the firing chart on page 14 (see *Firing Metal Clay with a Torch*, page 30). Allow the metal to cool completely. Burnish the pendant with a soft brass brush (see *Brush Burnishing*, page 31). Mix the epoxy according to the manufacturer's instructions. Mix blue ink into half of the epoxy and purple ink into the other half until you reach your desired colors. Using a toothpick, dab the epoxy onto the base of the pendant, being careful to avoid the raised circles. Here, I added blue to one half of the pendant and purple to the other half and swirled the two colors a bit in the middle of the pendant. Allow the epoxy to dry completely. Burnish the raised circles with the back of a metal spoon (see *Spoon Burnishing*, page 31).

tip

If you don't have an eraser to carve, use a bar of soap. It smells nice and, with a craft knife, it is very easy to carve.

Remember when, as a youngster in school, you were bored in class and you would write or carve pictures in those big pink erasers you took to school on the first day? Well, here is your chance to put that eraser art to work. Using a craft knife, you can carve a design into an eraser and make a perfect reversed stamp that will create a raised pattern on your clay. I suggest stocking up on erasers from your local dollar store so you can practice your carving skills. Erasers are a great medium to work with: when you become tired of the design, you can change it just by carving more out of the eraser.

MATERIALS

6g low-fire metal clay

metal clay slip or paste

eraser

small stir straw

metal spoon

basic metal clay tool kit (see page 17)

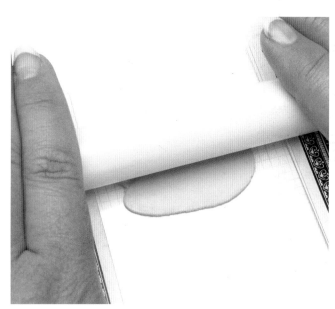

1. CARVE ERASER
Using the template for this project on page 126, carve an eraser with a craft knife. When cutting, angle the tip of the craft knife toward the center of each shape so that the stamp is beveled.

2. ROLL CLAY
Prepare your hands and work surface for working with metal clay (see *Handling Clay*, page 18). Roll metal clay to a five-card thickness (see *Rolling Clay*, page 19).

89

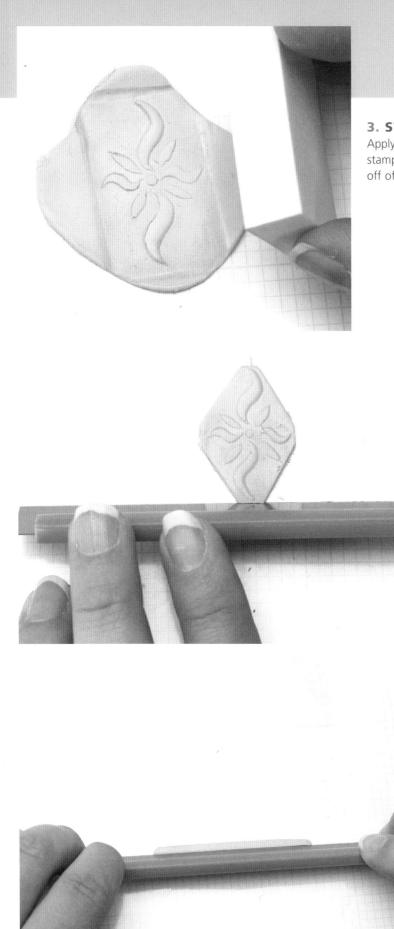

3. STAMP CLAY

Apply a thin layer of olive oil or beeswax balm to the eraser stamp. Press the stamp into the clay. Gently roll the stamp off of the clay.

4. TRIM CLAY

Using a straight blade, cut the clay around the stamped image. Allow the clay to dry completely and refine the edges of the piece (see *Refining Dry Clay*, page 29).

5. CUT CLAY FOR BAIL

Roll the remaining metal clay to a three-card thickness. Cut a ¼" × ¾" (6mm × 2cm) strip of clay.

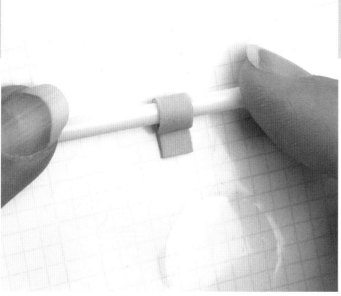

6. FORM BAIL

Lightly coat the stir straw with olive oil or beeswax balm. Form the clay strip into a tube bail with a tail around the stir straw (see *Creating a Tube Bail with a Tail*, page 27). Allow the bail to dry completely. Refine the edges of the bail.

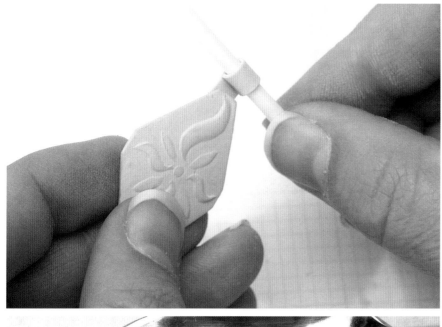

7. ATTACH BAIL

Join the bail to the stamped clay piece with metal clay paste (see *Layering Pieces of Clay*, page 24). Allow the clay to completely dry.

8. FIRE PENDANT

Fire the clay piece following the firing chart on page 14 (see *Firing Metal Clay with a Torch*, page 30). Allow the metal to cool completely. Burnish the pendant first with a soft brass brush, then with the back of a metal spoon (see *Burnishing*, page 31).

tip
Copper wire is great for making impression tools. With pliers, I bend 16- or 18-gauge wire into small shapes to use as stamps on metal clay.

The technique used to make this necklace is one of my favorites because the color and texture possibilities seem endless. You do not have to use bezel wire to make a bezel setting in metal clay pieces; you can make bezel settings in various shapes and sizes just by making a form out of a strip of metal clay. With the versatility of polymer clay, you can create just about any faux stone you want for your piece. In this project I have used a coiled copper wire stamp to texture both the metal clay and the polymer clay. Metallic paint provides beautiful color, along with a subtle sheen, to the translucent polymer clay. Try making several of these in different shapes and colors to match your wardrobe.

MATERIALS

7g low-fire metal clay

metal clay slip and paste

spiral stamp

small stir straw

translucent polymer clay

copper metallic paint (Posh Inkabilities)

22" (56cm) length of beading wire

2 sterling silver crimp tubes

1 sterling silver jump ring

1 sterling silver lobster claw clasp

32 size 6/0 gold seed beads

120 size 11/0 gold, brown and orange seed beads

16 brown bugle beads

14 gold bugle beads

basic metal clay tool kit (see page 17)

basic jewelry tool kit (see page 34)

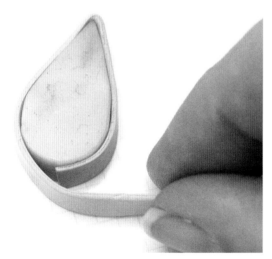

1. CREATE BEZEL

Condition a piece of polymer clay and roll it to a ¼" (6mm) thickness. Cut the polymer clay using the smaller template for this project on page 126. Bake the polymer clay piece according to the manufacturer's instructions. Allow the polymer clay piece to cool completely. Prepare your hands and work surface for working with metal clay (see *Handling Clay*, page 18). Roll the metal clay to a three-card thickness (see *Rolling Clay*, page 19). Cut the metal clay to ¼" × 3½" (6mm × 9cm). Apply a light coat of olive oil or beeswax balm to the polymer clay piece. Form the metal clay strip into a teardrop bezel around the polymer clay (see *Creating Bezels*, page 25). Allow the bezel to dry completely.

2. TEXTURE CLAY

Roll the remaining metal clay to a four-card thickness. Apply a thin layer of olive oil or beeswax balm to the spiral stamp. Press the rolled metal clay repeatedly with the spiral stamp. Cut the metal clay using the larger template for this project on page 126.

3. ATTACH BEZEL

Brush a line of water on the bottom rim of the bezel and on the base where the bezel will be located. Join the bezel to the base. Seal all of the edges where the clay joins.

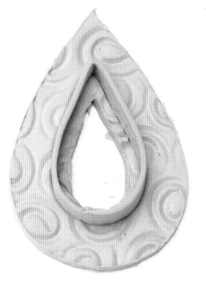

4. REMOVE CLAY

To make the pendant less heavy, cut out some of the metal clay inside of the bezel with a needle tool. Leave at least a ⅛" wide (3mm) lip of clay inside the bezel. Allow the clay to dry completely. Refine the inner and outer edges of the pendant and bezel (see *Refining Dry Clay*, page 29).

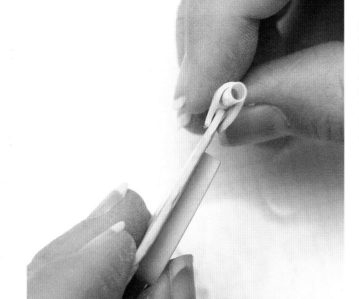

5. ATTACH BAIL

Roll the remaining metal clay to a three-card thickness. Cut the metal clay using the bail template for this project on page 126. Apply a thin layer of olive oil or beeswax balm to the small stir straw. Drape the clay over the straw for support and join the clay to the front and back of the pendant, forming a sandwich bail (see *Creating a Sandwich Bail*, page 27). Allow the clay to dry completely. Refine the edges of the bail.

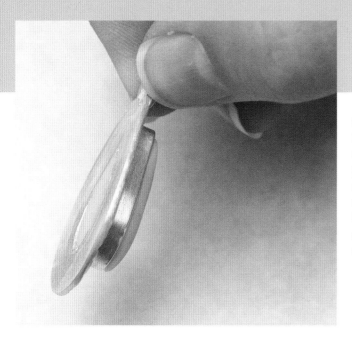

6. SHAPE POLYMER CLAY

Fire the pendant following the firing chart on page 14 (see *Firing Metal Clay with a Torch*, page 30). Allow the metal to cool completely. Burnish the pendant with a soft brass brush (see *Brush Burnishing*, page 31). Condition a piece of translucent polymer clay. Push the clay into the bezel, filling the bezel completely. Rock the clay on your work surface to shape it into a smooth cabochon. The clay should be level with the back of the pendant, with no clay protruding through the hole in the back.

7. TEXTURE CLAY

Press the spiral stamp into the polymer clay repeatedly, mimicking the texture in the metal clay. Bake the pendant, following the polymer clay manufacturer's instructions. Allow the pendant to cool completely.

8. FINISH NECKLACE

Rub copper metallic paint onto the surface of the baked polymer clay until you reach the color you desire. Allow the paint to dry. Attach the beading wire to the clasp with a crimp tube (see *Crimping*, page 37). String beads onto the wire in the following pattern: 1 gold size 6/0 seed bead, 2 size 11/0 seed beads, 1 brown bugle bead, 2 size 11/0 seed beads, 1 gold size 6/0 seed bead, 2 size 11/0 seed beads, 1 gold bugle bead, 2 size 11/0 seed beads. Repeat this pattern a total of 7 times, then string 1 gold size 6/0 seed bead, 2 size 11/0 seed beads, 1 brown bugle bead, 2 size 11/0 seed beads, and 1 gold size 6/0 seed bead. Slide the pendant onto the beading wire, and string the second half of the necklace, mirroring the first half. Crimp a jump ring onto the end of the necklace.

BRACELETS, RINGS
& OTHER THINGS

Bracelets have been commonly worn as jewelry for centuries. Bracelets come in many styles, such as bangles and charm bracelets, and can be made from materials from soft fabrics to hard metals and everything in between. They were popular long ago and still are today. If you have very young children, especially girls, you have probably seen just how fascinating bracelets are to them as they rifle through your jewelry box, putting on as many of them as their arms will allow.

Another popular piece of jewelry, rings, vary in size, color, purpose and artistic design. The most common shape is the circle. Rings also have been worn for centuries, and they have sometimes had symbolic meanings and uses. In Roman civilization, gold rings were permitted to freeborn citizens; silver, to freedmen; and iron, to slaves. The betrothal ring, used by Egyptians, Greeks and Romans, was adopted by early Christians, and later it evolved into the wedding ring. Throughout the ages, rings have been a part of history, culture and status among all types of societies.

This chapter has bracelet, ring, brooch and charm projects, all of which are as easy to make as they are attractive. From the hip *Free-Form Frenzy Ring* (page 106) to the lovely *Among the Stars Brooch* (page 112), these projects are fun to make and fun to wear. You will find in these projects several techniques that you can later expand on. Once you have made and worn some of these pieces I am sure the addiction will kick in and you will have a hankering to create more. So dig in, have fun and start puttin' on the glitz!

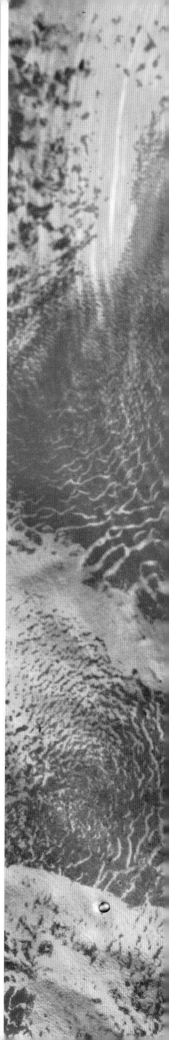

wearable words bracelet

Words are the key to communication and expression. Although it is usually said that a picture is worth a thousand words, sometimes a word can bring to mind a thousand pictures. One word that does that for me is *peace*. I am a huge fan of peace, whether it is on a physical, mental or spiritual level. I work toward having peace in my life on a daily basis, so it seemed only fitting for me to create a piece of jewelry that expresses my belief. Of course, you can use any word, or even a name, that is meaningful to you. After firing the metal clay, you can further highlight your expression with colored epoxy. So go ahead: Express yourself!

MATERIALS

3½g low-fire metal clay

alphabet rubber stamps

two-part epoxy (Loctite)

aqua metallic acrylic paint
   (Jacquard Lumiere)

11" (28cm) length of beading wire

4 sterling silver crimp tubes

5 sterling silver jump rings

1 sterling silver lobster claw clasp

approximately 75 size 8/0 aqua
   seed beads

basic metal clay tool kit (see page 17)

basic jewelry tool kit (see page 34)

tip

Use cloth hand wipes or baby wipes to clean your hands after completing each project, but don't throw the wipes away. Once dried, they can be used to rub metal clay pieces as a last step of refining.

1. STAMP CLAY

Prepare your hands and work surface for working with metal clay (see *Handling Clay*, page 18). Roll metal clay to a four-card thickness (see *Rolling Clay*, page 19). Apply a light coat of olive oil or beeswax balm to the alphabet rubber stamps and stamp the word of your choice into the clay.

2. FINISH METAL COMPONENT

Cut the metal clay around the stamped word. Here, I've cut the clay into a ⅜" × 1½" (1cm × 4cm) rectangle. Use a toothpick to create two holes at each end of the rectangle (see *Creating Holes in Wet Clay*, page 28). Allow the clay to dry completely, and refine the edges of the clay and the holes (see *Refining Dry Clay*, page 29). Fire the stamped clay following the firing chart on page 14 (see *Firing Metal Clay with a Torch*, page 30). Allow the metal to cool completely. Burnish the metal with a soft brass brush (see *Brush Burnishing*, page 31). Mix the epoxy according to the manufacturer's instructions. Mix the paint into the epoxy until you reach the color you desire (see *Adding Colored Two-Part Epoxy*, page 32). Using a toothpick, drip epoxy into the stamped letters. Allow the epoxy to dry completely.

3. BEGIN STRINGING BRACELET

Connect a jump ring to each of the four holes in the metal piece (see *Opening and Closing Jump Rings*, page 36). String 5 seed beads onto the beading wire and thread the beading wire through a jump ring on one end of the metal piece. String 3 more seed beads onto the beading wire, and thread the beading wire through the other jump ring on the same end of the metal piece.

4. COMPLETE BRACELET

String 5 more seed beads onto the beading wire. Adjust the beading wire so that 1" (3cm) of wire is on one side of the pair of jump rings and the remainder of the wire is on the other side. Thread both ends of the beading wire through a crimp tube and crimp the wires together (see *Crimping*, page 37). Trim the short wire's end. String 2½" (6cm) of seed beads onto the wire beyond the crimp tube and finish by crimping the clasp to the end of the wire. Repeat Steps 3 through 4 on the other side of the metal piece, crimping a jump ring onto the end of the wire instead of a clasp. To customize the length of this bracelet, adjust the beading wire length, or add more or fewer beads to each side of the metal clay piece.

fork it over bracelet

tip

For a design with several parallel lines, it is much easier to use a fork to create all the lines at one time, rather than create each line individually.

If you think forks are only for the dinner table, think again! This metal clay project gives you a whole new use for that age-old instrument. Even if you are not a geometry buff, you will enjoy making this easy, yet elegant, bracelet of squares and cubes. This project also shows you how to make a coordinating clasp that can be used on other metal clay projects, as well. String your finished metal clay components together with crystal cubes, and in no time you will have a beautiful bracelet to show off at the dinner table—and you won't even have to leave the kitchen!

MATERIALS

BRACELET

17g low-fire metal clay

metal clay paste

fork

metal spoon

14 sterling silver eye pins

4 5mm sterling silver jump rings

14 4mm orange crystal cube beads (Swarovski)

basic metal clay tool kit (see page 17)

basic jewelry tool kit (see page 34)

EARRING VARIATION

5g low-fire metal clay

fork

metal spoon

2 6mm magenta crystal cube beads (Swarovski)

2 sterling silver eye pins

2 sterling silver ear wires

basic metal clay tool kit (see page 17)

basic jewelry tool kit (see page 34)

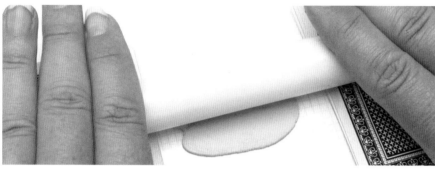

1. ROLL CLAY

Prepare your hands and work surface for working with metal clay (see *Handling Clay*, page 18). Roll metal clay to a four-card thickness (see Rolling Clay, page 19).

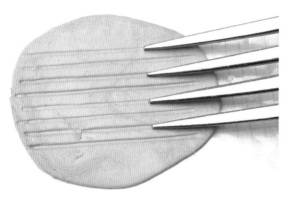

2. BEGIN PATTERNING CLAY

Drag the tines of a fork over the rolled clay once, then again between the first set of lines.

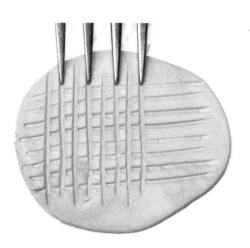

3. FINISH PATTERNING CLAY

Repeat Step 2, making lines perpendicular to the first set.

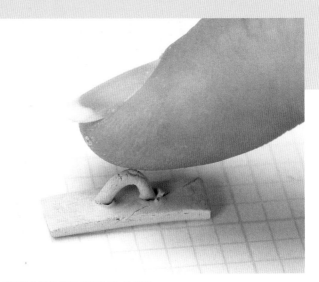

4. CUT CLAY

Cut 7 squares from the patterned clay using the large square template for this project on page 126. Cut the center out of 4 of the 7 clay squares using the small square template for this project on page 126.

5. CREATE TOGGLE BAR

Roll a small amount of metal clay to a five-card thickness. Cut a ¼" × ⅝" (6mm × 16mm) strip of clay. Using the tip of a pencil, make 2 small indentations in the strip, approximately ¼" (6mm) apart. Roll from metal clay a small snake, approximately 2mm in diameter and ⅜" (1cm) long. Use metal clay paste to join the snake to the back of the clay strip, placing the ends of the snake in the indentations (see *Layering Pieces of Clay*, page 24).

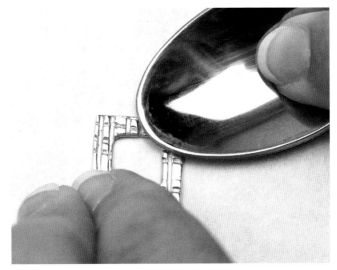

6. FINISH METAL CLAY COMPONENTS

Allow all of the metal clay pieces to dry thoroughly. Examine the join on the toggle bar, and strengthen it with paste if necessary. Refine the inner and outer edges of all of the pieces (see *Refining Dry Clay*, page 29). Compare all of the clay squares, filing if necessary until all pieces are the same size. Using a small drill bit or craft knife, drill 2 holes into one side of one of the open squares (see *Creating Holes in Dry Clay*, pg 28). This square will be the second half of the toggle clasp. Drill 4 holes in each of the remaining squares, 2 holes each on opposite sides. Fire the clay pieces individually following the firing chart on page 14 (see *Firing Metal Clay with a Torch*, page 30). Allow the metal to cool completely. Burnish the pieces first with a soft brass brush, then with the back of a metal spoon (see *Burnishing*, page 31).

7. ASSEMBLE BRACELET

Open the eye of an eye pin (see *Opening Ear Wires and Eye Pins*, page 36). Link the eye pin to the open square with only two holes. Slide a crystal bead onto the eye pin and close the free end of the eye pin with a loop (see *Creating Loops in Head Pins and Eye Pins*, page 37). Connect the empty loop of the eye pin to a closed metal square. Repeat, linking together all of the metal squares; alternate open squares with solid squares. Make a chain from the jump rings and use the chain to connect the toggle bar to the bracelet as shown above (see *Opening and Closing Jump Rings*, page 36).

To create matching earrings, prepare and mark the clay just as you did for the bracelet. Using the large square template for this project on page 126, cut two solid squares from the clay, then dry and refine the pieces. Compare the two pieces and file one if necessary to make them the same size. Drill a hole in a corner of each piece. Fire and burnish the pieces as you did for the bracelet. Link an eye pin to each metal square, and string a cube bead onto each eye pin. Close the open end of each eye pin with a loop, and link each dangle to an ear wire.

103

flower power charm bracelet

This project, might I say, is just charming (pun intended). This bracelet is a great look created with metal clay and bubble letters. After first designing this project using flower charms and glass leaf dangles, I thought it needed a little more pizzazz. As it happened, my daughter saw what I was making and wanted this piece for her own. Now, it's not often that a teenager will actually wear something that her mom makes, so I was happy to oblige; I decided to personalize it by adding her name. Adding the letter frames to the flowers and leaves really jazzes up this bracelet.

MATERIALS

21½g low-fire metal clay

metal clay slip and paste

lace doily

metal spoon

5mm sterling silver jump rings (2 for each letter in the name of your choice, plus 3 more)

1 sterling silver toggle clasp

⅜" (1cm) alphabet bubble stickers, to spell the name of your choice

glass leaf dangles (1 for each letter in the name of your choice, plus 1 more)

6" (15cm) length of sterling silver chain

basic metal clay tool kit (see page 17)

basic jewelry tool kit (see page 34)

tip

To speed up your cool down time after firing, you can use tweezers to pick up the hot metal clay and quench it in cold water. I use wood-handled cross-lock tweezers.

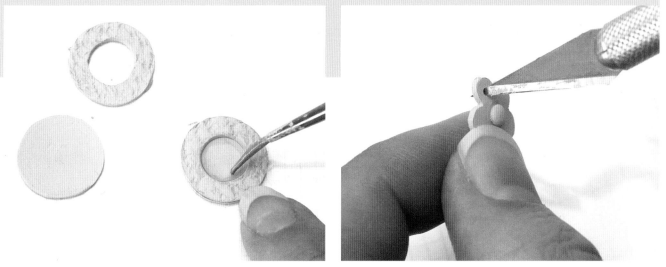

1. CREATE LETTER FRAMES

Prepare your hands and work surface for working with metal clay (see *Handling Clay*, page 18). Roll metal clay to a three-card thickness (see *Rolling Clay*, page 19). Press a lace doily into the clay to add texture. Cut 1 frame for each letter in the name of your choice using the outer and inner lines of the circle template for this project on page 126. Dry the clay frames, and refine the inner edges of the frames (see *Refining Dry Clay*, page 29). Roll the remaining metal clay to a three-card thickness. Cut 1 base circle for each frame using the outer line only of the round template for this project on page 126. Join each clay frame to a base circle (see *Layering Pieces of Clay*, page 24).

2. CREATE FLOWERS

Roll the remaining metal clay to a four-card thickness. Using the flower template for this project on page 126, cut out 1 flower for each letter frame plus 1 additional flower. Roll a small ball of metal clay and join it to the center of a clay flower; repeat for each flower. Allow all of the letter frames and flowers to dry completely. Refine the edges of each metal clay piece. Compare the like clay pieces to ensure they are the same size. If the like pieces are not the same size, file the larger pieces until each piece is the same size. Using a small drill bit or craft knife, drill a hole in each letter frame and flower (see *Creating Holes in Dry Clay*, page 28).

3. COMPLETE LETTER FRAMES

Fire each clay piece following the firing chart on page 14 (see *Firing Metal Clay with a Torch*, page 30). Allow the metal to cool completely. Burnish the metal first with a soft brass brush, then with the back of a metal spoon (see *Burnishing*, page 31). Attach the alphabet stickers for the name of your choice to the letter frames.

4. ASSEMBLE BRACELET

Using jump rings, attach a piece of the toggle clasp to each end of the silver chain (see *Opening and Closing Jump Rings*, page 36). With a jump ring, attach a flower to the first link in the chain. Attach a leaf dangle to the same link, opposite the flower. Skip 2 links and attach the first letter frame to the silver chain with a jump ring. Continue attaching flowers, leaves and letter frames across the length of the bracelet, ending on a flower and leaf dangle.

free-form frenzy ring

This is a hip, free-form ring that is easy to customize to the wearer. This ring does not connect to form a full circle, so it can be adjusted to fit. I decorated the top of this ring with chopped pieces of dried metal clay, which I like to call "crunchies." To create your crunchies, you can purposely dry out a small piece of clay. Otherwise, since there are no mistakes in metal clay work, only opportunities, you can take this opportunity to recycle dried clay from projects that didn't turn out as you had intended to create your crunchies.

MATERIALS

5½g low-fire metal clay
metal clay slip and paste
small stir straw
ring form (see *Creating Rings*, page 26)
metal spoon
basic metal clay tool kit (see page 17)

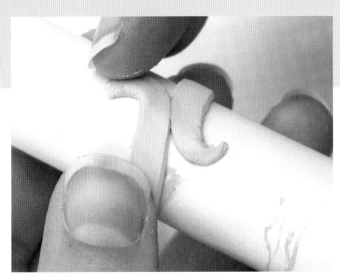

1. FORM RING

Prepare your hands and work surface for working with metal clay (see *Handling Clay*, page 18). Roll metal clay to a five-card thickness (see *Rolling Clay*, page 19). Cut a ¼"-wide (6mm) strip of clay to a length equal to your desired ring circumference plus 1" (3cm) (see *Creating Rings*, page 26). Taper each end of the strip. Apply a thin coat of olive oil or beeswax balm to the ring form. Wrap the clay strip around the ring form, but do not allow the clay strip to touch itself. Curl the tapered ends of the strip outward. Allow the clay to dry completely. Refine the edges of the ring, slightly beveling each edge so that the ring will be comfortable to wear after firing (see *Refining Dry Clay*, page 29).

2. CREATE EMBELLISHMENTS

Roll the remaining metal clay to a two-card thickness. Using the small stir straw as a template, cut two small circles from the rolled clay. Cut a ½" × ½" (13mm × 13mm) square from the rolled clay. Allow the square and circles to dry completely. Refine the edges of the small circles. Using a straight blade, chop up the dried clay square into coarse grains.

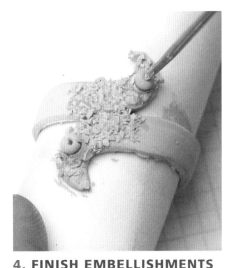
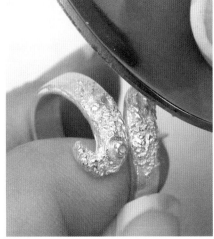

3. EMBELLISH RING

Brush the ends of the ring with paste. Roll the ring in the dried clay grains. Brush a thin layer of water over the grains to bond them to the ring.

4. FINISH EMBELLISHMENTS

Join 1 small clay circle to each end of the ring (see *Layering Pieces of Clay*, page 24). Roll 2 small balls of metal clay and join them to the small circles. Indent each ball of clay with the tip of a needle tool. Allow the clay to dry completely. File any remaining rough edges.

5. FIRE RING

Fire the ring following the firing chart on page 14 (see *Firing Metal Clay with a Torch*, page 30). Allow the metal to cool completely. Burnish the metal first with a soft brass brush, then with the back of a metal spoon (see *Burnishing*, page 31).

berry original ring

tip

Take time to experiment with liver of sulfur. For example: After you dip a piece in liver of sulfur, brass brush the entire piece or just a few areas, then dip the piece again. Spritzing a piece with ammonia before dipping the piece will result in a multicolored patina. And remember, if you don't like the way the patina looks, heat the piece with a torch to remove all of the patina, then try again.

Rings are an important part of my jewelry repertoire. I enjoy wearing rings and changing them to match my outfits. For this dainty design, I cut out a few leaf shapes and used a needle tool for the vein work. I then added a few berries, and soon I had an eye-catching ring. This ring was beautiful just after firing, but I decided to further enhance its beauty with liver of sulfur, which creates a wonderful patina on fine silver. Why not try your hand at creating this lovely ring for yourself?

MATERIALS

6g low-fire metal clay

metal clay slip and paste

ring form (see *Creating Rings*, page 26)

metal spoon

liver of sulfur

baking soda

2 glass containers

polishing cloth

basic metal clay tool kit (see page 17)

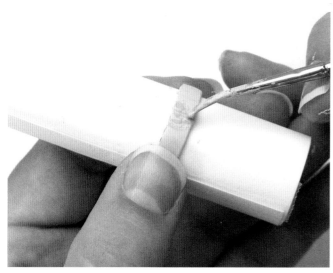

1. FORM RING

Prepare your hands and work surface for working with metal clay (see *Handling Clay*, page 18). Roll metal clay to a five-card thickness (see *Rolling Clay*, page 19). Cut a ¼" × 4" (6mm × 10cm) strip of clay. Apply a thin coat of olive oil or beeswax balm to the ring form; join the metal clay strip into a ring around the ring form, trimming the strip so that the ends touch but don't overlap (see *Creating Rings*, page 26). Allow the clay to dry completely. Refine the inner and outer edges of the ring, slightly beveling each edge so that the ring will be comfortable to wear after firing (see *Refining Dry Clay*, page 29). Sand and fill the join as needed until the ring appears seamless.

2. CREATE LEAVES

Roll the remaining metal clay to a three-card thickness. Cut freehand 6 small leaves from the rolled clay. Use the tip of a needle tool to draw veins onto the leaves.

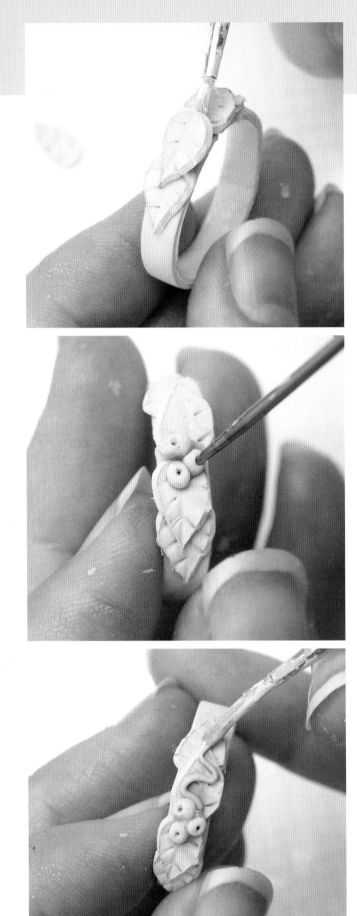

3. JOIN LEAVES TO RING

Join 1 leaf to the ring over the seam (see *Layering Pieces of Clay*, page 24). Join the second leaf to the ring ½" (13mm) from the first leaf, with the wide ends of the leaves toward each other. Join the second layer of leaves on top of the first, about ¼" (6mm) apart. Join the fifth leaf to the ring, overlapping one of the leaves in the second layer. Join the last leaf to the ring, slightly overlapping the fifth leaf.

4. ATTACH BERRIES

Roll 3 small balls of metal clay. Join these clay berries to the ring at the point where the fifth and sixth leaves overlap. Indent each berry with the point of a needle tool. Brush the berries with slip for extra strength.

5. COMPLETE RING

Roll a small snake of metal clay, approximately 2mm in diameter and ¼" (6mm) long. Join the clay snake in a squiggle shape next to the berries. Brush the clay snake with slip for extra strength.

6. FIRE RING

Fire the ring following the firing chart on page 14 (see *Firing Metal Clay with a Torch*, page 30). Allow the metal to cool completely. Burnish the metal first with a soft brass brush, then with the back of a metal spoon (see *Burnishing*, page 31).

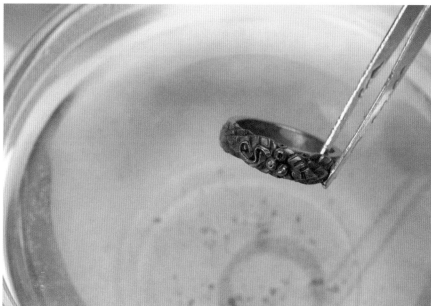

7. PATINATE RING

Patinate the ring using liver of sulfur (see *Using Liver of Sulfur*, page 33).

8. POLISH RING

Using a polishing cloth, remove the patina from the raised elements of the ring.

among the stars brooch

I love creating fanciful stars that look as if they are reaching out and dangling their wishes overhead. These stars remind me of nursery rhymes because the stars appear so innocent, with a childlike serenity. You can make a wish upon your own star with this shining brooch. Use a rubber stamp of your choice to texture the large star and a nylon scrub pad to texture the small star. I also added Swarovski crystal beads to complement the brooch. This project may just become the star of your wardrobe!

MATERIALS

7g low-fire metal clay

floral rubber stamp

nylon scrub pad

metal spoon

two-part epoxy (Loctite)

1 sterling silver eye pin

1 pin back

2 4mm blue crystal bicone beads (Swarovski)

1 4mm clear crystal bicone bead (Swarovski)

basic metal clay tool kit (see page 17)

basic jewelry tool kit (see page 34)

1. STAMP CLAY

Prepare your hands and work surface for working with metal clay (see *Handling Clay*, page 18). Roll metal clay to a four-card thickness (see *Rolling Clay*, page 19). Apply a light coat of olive oil or beeswax balm to the rubber stamp. Press the rubber stamp into the rolled clay.

2. CUT CLAY

Using the large star template for this project on page 126, cut the stamped clay. Allow the metal clay star to dry completely. Refine all of the edges of the star (see *Refining Dry Clay*, page 29). Using a small drill bit or craft knife, drill a hole in one of the star's points (see *Creating Holes in Dry Clay*, page 28).

3. CREATE STAR DANGLE

Roll the remaining metal clay to a four-card thickness. Dab the rolled metal clay with a nylon scrub pad for texture. Using the small star template for this project on page 126, cut a small star from the textured clay. Allow the metal clay star to dry completely. Refine all of the edges of the star. Using a small drill bit or craft knife, drill a hole in one of the star's points. Be especially careful not to drill the hole too close to the edge of the clay.

4. JOIN STARS

Fire the stars individually following the firing chart on page 14 (see *Firing Metal Clay with a Torch*, page 30). Allow the pieces to cool completely. Burnish the metal first with a soft brass brush, then with the back of a metal spoon (see *Burnishing*, page 31). Connect an eye pin to the small star (see *Opening Ear Wires and Eye Pins*, page 36). Slide a blue crystal bicone, a clear crystal bicone, then a blue crystal bicone onto the eye pin. Make a loop in the end off the eye pin (see *Creating Loops in Head Pins and Eye Pins*, page 37). Hook the loop through the hole in the large star, then close the loop.

5. ATTACH PIN BACK

Mix the two-part epoxy according to the manufacturer's instructions. With the epoxy, adhere the pin back to the large star. Allow the epoxy to dry completely.

crazy daisy brooch

tip

I suggest sanding and refining your clay piece before making any holes in it. This way, you will have a better idea of how close to the edge you need to drill.

The idea for this unique brooch just popped out at me one day. I love flowers, and they are not just a summer item; they span the whole year. There are spring, summer, fall and winter flowers, and you can tailor this project to whichever season you prefer. I decided I wanted to add a little spring action to this project for a fun twist; I was able to accomplish that with a coiled wire stem. A little bit of two-part epoxy completes this piece with a hint of color. Let your creativity bloom and create a brooch that any butterfly would be happy to land on!

MATERIALS

12g low-fire metal clay

metal clay slip and paste

cap from a 2-liter bottle

spiral stamp

two-part epoxy (Loctite)

yellow ink (Adirondack Alcohol Ink)

green ink (Adirondack Alcohol Ink)

8" (20cm) length of green 22-gauge
    copper wire (Artistic Wire Ltd.)

1 pin back

basic metal clay tool kit (see page 17)

basic jewelry tool kit (see page 34)

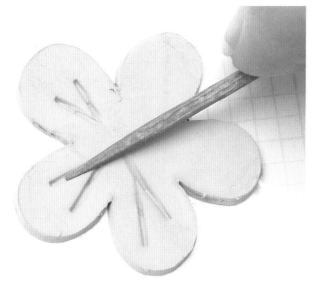 

1. CREATE FLOWER
Prepare your hands and work surface for working with metal clay (see *Handling Clay*, page 18). Roll metal clay to a four-card thickness (see *Rolling Clay*, page 19). Cut the clay into a flower shape using the template for this project on page 126. Use the tip of a toothpick to indent 2 lines on each petal of the flower.

2. EMBELLISH FLOWER
Roll a pea-size ball of metal clay and join it to the center of the clay flower (see *Layering Pieces of Clay*, page 24). Make several indentations in the ball of clay with a toothpick to imitate the appearance of the center of a daisy.

115

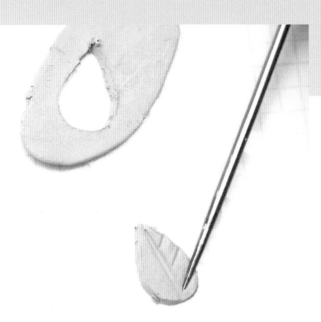

3. CREATE LEAF

Roll the remaining metal clay to a three-card thickness. Cut free-hand a small leaf, approximately ½" (1cm) long, from the rolled clay. Use the tip of a needle tool to draw veins onto the leaf.

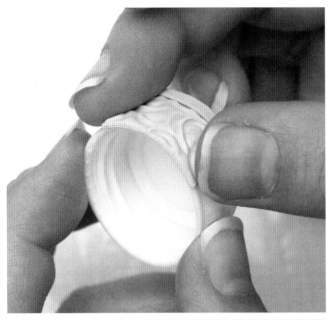

4. BEGIN FLOWERPOT

Roll the remaining metal clay to a four-card thickness. Apply a thin layer of olive oil or beeswax balm to a spiral stamp. Stamp the rolled metal clay repeatedly with the spiral stamp. Cut the metal clay to 1" × ⅝" (3cm × 2cm). Roll the remaining metal clay to a two-card thickness. Cut a 1" × ⅛" (3cm × 3mm) strip of clay. Join this clay strip to the top long edge of the textured clay rectangle. Place the clay rectangle on the bottle cap and allow the clay to dry in a curved shape.

5. COMPLETE FLOWERPOT

Roll the remaining metal clay to a four-card thickness. Using the curved rectangle as a template, cut the rolled clay to form the back of the flowerpot. Stand the curved piece upright, and use the curve as a template to cut a piece of metal clay for the bottom of the flowerpot. Using metal clay paste, join the front, back and bottom of the flowerpot together. Allow all of the clay pieces to dry completely and refine the edges of each piece (see *Refining Dry Clay*, page 29). Using a small drill bit or craft knife, drill a hole into the clay leaf (see *Creating Holes in Dry Clay*, page 28).

6. ADD TINTED EPOXY

Fire the clay pieces individually following the firing chart on page 14 (see *Firing Metal Clay with a Torch*, page 30). Allow the pieces to cool completely. Burnish the metal with a soft brass brush (see *Brush Burnishing*, page 31). Mix two-part epoxy according to the manufacturer's instructions. Stir yellow ink into the epoxy and dab it onto the center of the metal daisy with a toothpick (see *Adding Colored Two-Part Epoxy*, page 32). Allow the epoxy to dry completely.

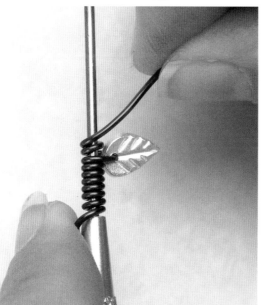

7. COIL WIRE

Hold down the first ¼" (6mm) of the green wire on the handle of a needle tool. Begin coiling the rest of the wire around the tip of the needle tool. After the coil is ¼" (6mm) long, string the metal leaf onto the wire. Continue coiling the wire until the coil is ⅝" (2cm) long. Trim the remaining wire, leaving a ¼" (6mm) tail. Mix two-part epoxy according to the manufacturer's instructions. Stir green ink into the epoxy and dab it into the veins of the leaf. Allow the epoxy to dry completely.

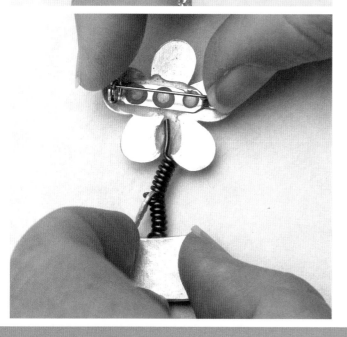

8. ASSEMBLE PIN

Mix two-part epoxy according to the manufacturer's instructions. Adhere 1 end of the coiled wire inside of the flowerpot and the other end to the back of the daisy. Attach the pin back to the back of the daisy with epoxy, as well. Allow the epoxy to dry completely.

welcoming wine charms

You can attach these hoops to any stemware for easy beverage identification, but you do not have to be a wine drinker to enjoy this simple project. These delightful little charms can pull double duty as earrings, as well, because they are created using beading hoops. You can make a matching set, then after your party you can wear them to your next gathering. I used a rubber alphabet stamp to adorn the metal clay, but the possibilities are endless when designing these charming charms.

MATERIALS

1g low-fire metal clay for each wine charm

alphabet rubber stamp

1 ¾ " (2cm) sterling silver beading hoop for each wine charm

2 sterling silver crimp tubes for each wine charm

1 sterling silver jump ring for each wine charm

8 size 8/0 seed beads for each wine charm

2 3mm sterling silver beads for each wine charm

basic metal clay tool kit (see page 17)

basic jewelry tool kit (see page 34)

1. STAMP CLAY

Prepare your hands and work surface for working with metal clay (see *Handling Clay*, page 18). Roll metal clay to a five-card thickness (see *Rolling Clay*, page 19). Apply a light layer of olive oil or beeswax balm to the alphabet rubber stamp and press it into the rolled clay.

2. CUT CLAY

Using a straight blade, cut the clay into a square around the stamped image. Using a toothpick or needle tool, make a hole in the corner of the clay piece (see *Creating Holes in Wet Clay*, page 28).

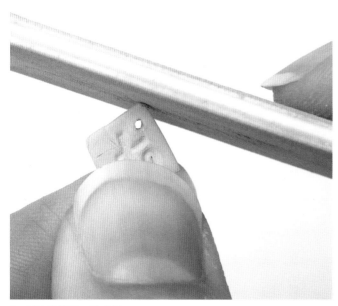

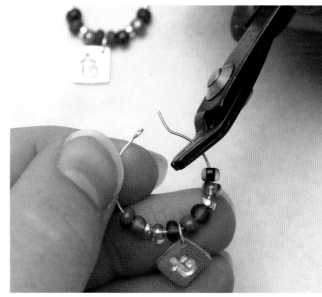

3. REFINE CLAY

Allow the metal clay square to dry completely. Refine the edges of the dried clay and round the corners (see *Refining Dry Clay*, page 29). Refine the hole in the clay square with the tip of a craft knife.

4. ASSEMBLE WINE CHARMS

Repeat Steps 1 through 3 for each wine charm. Fire the wine charms individually following the firing chart on page 14 (see *Firing Metal Clay with a Torch*, page 30). Allow the pieces to cool completely. Burnish the metal with a soft brass brush (see *Brush Burnishing*, page 31). For each wine charm, hook a jump ring through the hole in the metal square (see *Opening and Closing Jump Rings*, page 36). Slide 1 crimp tube, 2 seed beads, 1 silver bead, 2 seed beads, the metal charm, 2 seed beads, 1 silver bead, 2 seed beads and 1 crimp tube onto the beading hoop. To finish, push all of the beads together and crimp the crimp tubes (see *Crimping*, page 37).

Gallery

Inspiration! Sometimes that is all you need to fuel your inner artist. And now that you have a few projects and a few techniques under your belt, you can look at jewelry in a whole new light. Just knowing the possibilities and options available to you in metal clay is inspiration enough. I have included some works of art in this gallery section to show you how you can take your jewelry creations a step further. I hope these pieces inspire you to continue on your metal clay journey.

< Shown top to bottom, left to right:

Dichroic Pendant
by Tammy Garner
Metal clay and dichroic glass cabochon by Ernie Downey

Autumn Creek Earrings
by Tammy Garner
Metal clay with Aura 22 gold highlights and liver of sulfur patina

Organic Frantic Bracelet
by Tammy Garner
Stamped metal clay with cubic zirconia and brecciated jasper

Fused Glass Striped Pendant
by Ernie Downey
Metal clay, fused glass and cubic zirconia

Blue Lentil Earrings
by Tammy Garner
Metal clay with liver of sulfur patina, fine silver highlights and Swarovski crystal

Gold Swirl Earrings
by Tammy Garner
Stamped metal clay with Aura 22 gold highlights

< Continued from page 120:
Funky Face Brooch
by Tammy Garner
Metal clay with colored pencil drawing,
two-part epoxy and colored copper wire

Purple Eye Pendant
by Tammy Garner
Metal clay with fine silver wire and
purple cubic zirconia

> Shown top to bottom, left to right:
Ethereal Pool
by Hollie J. Mion
Metal clay with glass enamel

Fused Glass Pendant
by Tammy Garner
Metal clay with fused glass and cubic
zirconia

Faith Flame Pendant
by Tammy Garner
Metal clay with cubic zirconia

Dotted Disk Earrings
by Tammy Garner
Metal clay with cubic zirconia and
Swarovski crystal

CZ Ring
by Tammy Garner
Metal clay with cubic zirconia

Felix the Cat Brooch
by Tammy Garner
Stamped metal clay with two-part epoxy

Cross Pendant
by Tammy Garner
Metal clay with cubic zirconia and liver
of sulfur patina

My Deep Blue Pond
by Hollie J. Mion
Metal clay with fine silver bezel and opal

< Shown top to bottom, left to right:

Flaming Heart Brooch
by Tammy Garner
Metal clay fired over cork clay for a hollow form with liver of sulfur patina

Moon Shell Necklace
by Tammy Garner
Molded metal clay and jet shells

Copper Wave Earrings
by Tammy Garner
Metal clay with copper wire and graduated liver of sulfur patina

> Shown top to bottom, left to right:

Bomb Earrings
by Tammy Garner
*Stamped metal clay with liver of sulfur
patina*

Silver and Glass Bracelet
by Tammy Garner
*Metal clay, polymer clay and glass
beads*

Lentil Pie Pendant
by Tammy Garner
*Hollow metal clay with liver of sulfur
patina*

Geo-Copper Earrings
by Tammy Garner
*Stamped metal clay with liver of sulfur
patina, ribbon and copper wire*

Tornado's Eye Pendant
by Tammy Garner
*Stamped metal clay with liver of sulfur
patina and cubic zirconia*

Resources

There are many suppliers of metal clay products and accessories. Below I have listed a few of my favorite resources that will help you with both information and supplies if you are not able to find what you need locally.

METAL CLAY INFORMATION, ORGANIZATIONS & GUILDS

Art Clay World USA, Inc.

(866) 381-0100 x102

www.artclayworld.com

Technical information, class listings, instructor listings, certification program, tips and techniques

National Polymer Clay Guild

www.npcg.org

Information on classes, events, seminars, instructors and local guilds

PMC Guild

www.pmcguild.com

Technical information, class listings, instructor listings and tips

METAL CLAY SUPPLIES

Fire Mountain Gems and Beads

(800) 355-2137

www.firemountaingems.com

PMC Connection

(866) PMC-CLAY

www.pmcconnection.com

Certification program

PMC Supply

(800) 388-2001

www.pmcsupply.com

www.artclaysupply.com

Rio Grande

(800) 545-6566

www.riogrande.com

Certification program

Whole Lotta Whimsy

(520) 531-1966

www.wholelottawhimsy.com

POLYMER CLAY, INKS, PAINTS, EPOXY & WIRE

Artistic Wire Ltd.

(630) 530-7567

www.artisticwire.com

Colored wire, wire-shaping tools, books and videos

Henkel Corporation

Loctite products

(860) 571-5100

www.loctite.com

Epoxy kits

Jacquard Products

Rupert, Gibbon & Spider, Inc.

(800) 442-0455

www.jacquardproducts.com

Lumiere paints, Piñata colors, Pearl Ex powdered pigments, accessories

Polyform Products

(847) 427-0020

www.sculpey.com

Sculpey, Premo!, Granitex, kits and accessories

Ranger Industries

(732) 389-3535

www.rangerink.com

Nonstick craft sheets, Mold-n-Pour, Perfect Pearls Pigment powders, Posh Impressions Metallic Inkabilities inks, paints, tools and accessories

BEADS & JEWELRY FINDINGS

Fire Mountain Gems and Beads

(800) 355-2137

www.firemountaingems.com

Beads, sterling silver findings, instructions, tools and stringing supplies

Rings & Things

(800) 366-2156

www.rings-things.com

Beads, sterling silver findings, instructions, tools and stringing supplies

Rio Grande

(800) 545-6566

www.riogrande.com

Beads, sterling silver findings, instructions, tools and stringing supplies

TOOLS

Contenti

(401) 305-3000

www.contenti.com

Pliers, drills, brushes, tweezers, scales and more

LUBRICATING BALM

W.S. Badger Company

(800) 603-6100

www.badgerbalm.com

For the best in olive oil hand balms and other all-natural body care products

tammy's handmade balm recipe

2 TABLESPOONS OLIVE OIL

1 TABLESPOON BEESWAX (CAN BE REPLACED WITH AN ADDITIONAL 1 TABLESPOON SOYWAX)

1 TABLESPOON SOYWAX (CAN BE REPLACED WITH AN ADDITIONAL 1 TABLESPOON BEESWAX AND 1 TEASPOON OLIVE OIL)

2 TEASPOONS EVENING PRIMROSE OIL (OPTIONAL)

1 CAPSULE VITAMINE E (OPTIONAL)

1 CAPSULE ALOE VERA (OPTIONAL)

5 DROPS LAVENDER OIL OR ESSENTIAL OIL OF YOUR CHOICE (OPTIONAL)

SHALLOW CONTAINER WITH LARGE OPENING, SUCH AS A SMALL TIN FROM CANDIES OR MINTS

Melt the first 6 ingredients together in a small double boiler over medium heat. Add the lavender oil or essential oil. Mix well and pour into the container you have chosen.

Templates

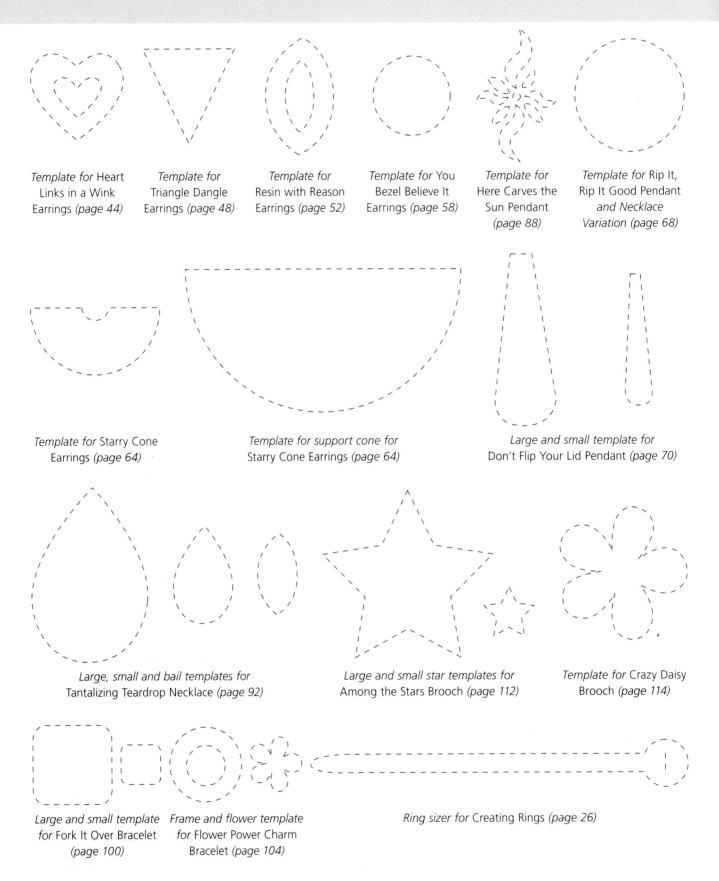

Template for Heart Links in a Wink Earrings *(page 44)*

Template for Triangle Dangle Earrings *(page 48)*

Template for Resin with Reason Earrings *(page 52)*

Template for You Bezel Believe It Earrings *(page 58)*

Template for Here Carves the Sun Pendant *(page 88)*

Template for Rip It, Rip It Good Pendant and Necklace Variation *(page 68)*

Template for Starry Cone Earrings *(page 64)*

Template for support cone for Starry Cone Earrings *(page 64)*

Large and small template for Don't Flip Your Lid Pendant *(page 70)*

Large, small and bail templates for Tantalizing Teardrop Necklace *(page 92)*

Large and small star templates for Among the Stars Brooch *(page 112)*

Template for Crazy Daisy Brooch *(page 114)*

Large and small template for Fork It Over Bracelet *(page 100)*

Frame and flower template for Flower Power Charm Bracelet *(page 104)*

Ring sizer for Creating Rings *(page 26)*

Index

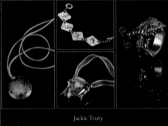